F-22A Raptor 03-4058 from the 27th Fighter Squadron 'Fighting Eagles' fires an AIM-120 Advanced Medium Range Air-to-Air Missile (AMRAAM) during a Combat Archer mission. US Air Force/Master Sergeant Michael Ammons

# CONTENTS

ISBN: 978 1 80282 815 3
Editor: Jon Lake
Senior editor, specials: Roger Mortimer
Email: roger.mortimer@keypublishing.com
Cover Design: Steve Donovan
Design: SJmagic DESIGN SERVICES, India
Advertising Sales Manager: Brodie Baxter
Email: brodie.baxter@keypublishing.com
Tel: 01780 755131
Advertising Production:
Becky Antoniades
Email: Rebecca.antoniades@keypublishing.com

SUBSCRIPTION/MAIL ORDER
Key Publishing Ltd, PO Box 300, Stamford, Lincs, PE9 1NA
Tel: 01780 480404
Subscriptions email:
subs@keypublishing.com

Mail Order email: orders@keypublishing.com
Website: www.keypublishing.com/shop

PUBLISHING
Group CEO and Publisher: Adrian Cox

Published by
Key Publishing Ltd, PO Box 100, Stamford, Lincs, PE9 1XQ
Tel: 01780 755131
Website: www.keypublishing.com

PRINTING
Precision Colour Printing Ltd, Haldane, Halesfield 1, Telford, Shropshire. TF7 4QQ

DISTRIBUTION
Seymour Distribution Ltd, 2 Poultry Avenue, London, EC1A 9PU
Enquiries Line: 02074 294000.

KEY Publishing

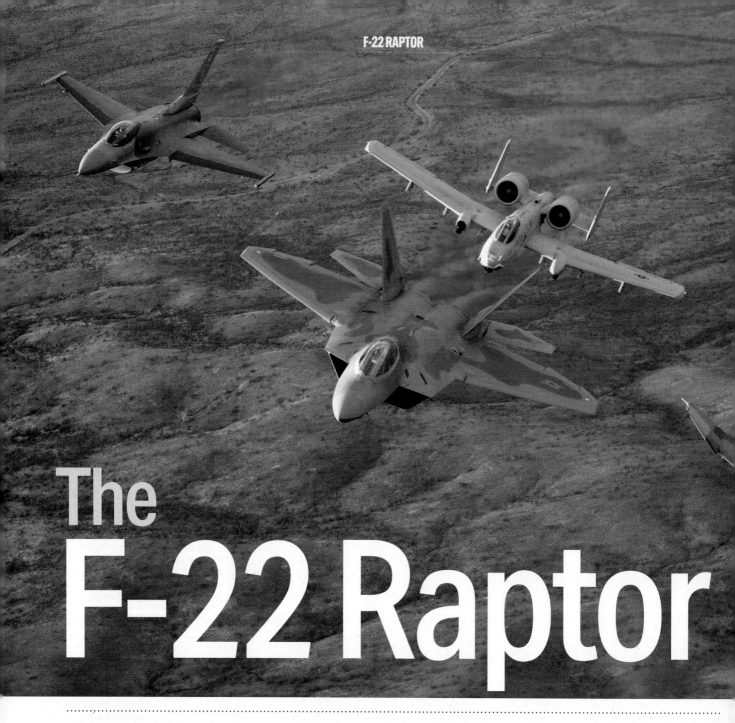

# The F-22 Raptor

The Lockheed Martin F-22A Raptor is widely acknowledged as being the pre-eminent air-to-air fighter in the world today. The type has racked up an unmatched kill: loss ratio on exercise and won an enviable reputation for literally unbeatable combat effectiveness. And yet, at the same time, the F-22A is massively expensive, its production has been cut back again and again, and it now faces a retirement that some believe is premature, while others question the relevance of the aircraft to modern operations.

Lockheed Martin coined the term 'fifth generation fighter' to describe the F-22A. The company defined it as a fighter that encompassed 'designed in' advanced 'stealth' (low observability, especially to radar), extreme performance, sensor/information fusion and advanced sustainment. Before it also needed to apply the 'fifth generation' tag to the F-35 Joint Strike Fighter, Lockheed Martin specifically included supercruise performance (the ability to achieve and maintain speeds in excess of Mach 1.5 for extended periods of time without the use of afterburners) and extreme agility as being key 'fifth generation' defining features too.

Uniquely among the world's in-service fighters, the F-22 has all of these features, conferring a quantum leap in lethality and survivability and making it arguably the world's only true 'fifth generation' fighter.

It is certainly the United States' premier fighter aircraft – an air power tool that has become essential to America's national security.

And the F-22A's superiority over all other fighter aircraft is tacitly acknowledged even by rival manufacturers. Such rivals no longer claim to offer 'the best', but instead compete to claim that their fighters are second only to the Raptor! The degree of superiority enjoyed by the F-22A is such that it is described as an Air Dominance Fighter. Such a tag has been validated by the Raptor's performance in successive exercises.

During Exercise Northern Edge in Alaska in June 2006, a small force of 12 F-22s downed 108 adversaries with no losses in simulated air combat. In a subsequent Northern Edge exercise in January 2007, F-22s scored 144 simulated kills, again with no losses. In its first participation in a Red Flag exercise in February

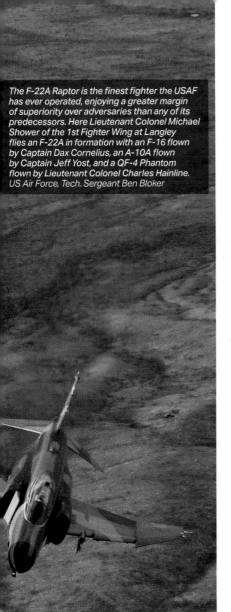

The F-22A Raptor is the finest fighter the USAF has ever operated, enjoying a greater margin of superiority over adversaries than any of its predecessors. Here Lieutenant Colonel Michael Shower of the 1st Fighter Wing at Langley flies an F-22A in formation with an F-16 flown by Captain Dax Cornelius, an A-10A flown by Captain Jeff Yost, and a QF-4 Phantom flown by Lieutenant Colonel Charles Hainline. US Air Force, Tech. Sergeant Ben Bloker

Flying the Raptor is a highly prized posting for young USAF pilots, who are something of an elite. Here, an F-22 pilot from the 149th Fighter Squadron, part of the Virginia Air National Guard's 192nd Fighter Wing, looks over a pre-flight checklist with his aircraft's crew chief, during Exercise Northern Edge 2015 at Joint Base Elmendorf Richardson, Alaska, on June 15, 2015. US Air Force, Staff Sergeant Jonathan Garcia

2007, the F-22A rapidly established air dominance, annihilating the defending forces without loss. During an Operational Readiness Inspection (ORI) in April 2008, the F-22A scored 221 simulated kills, while suffering no losses. Occasional victories against the F-22A have been recorded, but these are viewed as being newsworthy events, and have only served to further enhance the F-22A's formidable reputation.

So, what makes the F-22A such a difficult opponent in air-to-air combat?

At root, the factors that define the Raptor as a fifth generation fighter are those which make it so hard to beat. 'Low Observable' or Stealth characteristics make the F-22 extremely difficult to detect. This combination means that F-22 pilots can see the enemy but cannot be seen themselves. Stealth gives the Raptor pilot the ability to pick and choose where, when, and even whether he engages the threat, all the while remaining virtually undetected by enemy air defences.

Supercruise enhances survivability and lethality by allowing the F-22A pilot to perform his mission faster, with less exposure to enemy defences, and to rapidly engage distant, time-critical targets, and to do so without incurring massive penalties in range. The combination of stealth and supercruise dramatically shrinks enemy surface-to-air missile engagement envelopes, giving the advantage of surprise, while reducing an enemy's opportunity to track and engage

Most air to air photos of the F-22 are taken from an accompanying tanker – there is no two-seat version and wingmen usually stay at the limit of visual range. Nor do operational Raptors bristle with weapons – as these are carried internally. But this picture does show an F-22A refuelling from a US Air Force KC-10 Extender during the type's first wartime mission, on September 26, 2014, operating as part of a strike package tasked with engaging IS targets in Syria. US Air Force, Technical Sergeant Russ Scalf

*Major Paul 'Loco' Lopez was responsible for showing off the Raptor's agility as the primary pilot on the F-22 Raptor Demonstration Team. The relatively confined dimensions of the F-22 canopy have complicated efforts to integrate a modern helmet mounted sighting system. US Air Force*

*Above and below: Massive tailerons, plentiful specific excess power, thrust vectoring and a sophisticated fly by wire control system provide the F-22 with unmatched agility, while the 35,000lb of afterburning thrust from each of the two Pratt & Whitney F119-PW-100 augmented turbofan engines allows a rapid recovery of energy. Supermanoeuvrability was one of the key defining features of Lockheed Martin's original definition of fifth generation capability. US Air Force*

the F-22. This will often mean that by the time the F-22 is detected, it's too late to do anything about it!

Extreme agility, conferred by the aircraft's large control surfaces and thrust-vectoring nozzles, allows the F-22 to outmanoeuvre and out-accelerate any threat. The Russian fighters that pioneered super-manoeuvrability and thrust-vectoring were dismissed as being impressive air show performers, whose agility promised to be a potentially useful 'last ditch' defensive capability, but one that was inevitably accompanied by a potentially catastrophic loss of energy. The F-22A enjoys a much better ability to regain energy rapidly.

The Raptor pilot has advanced integrated avionics, which process data from an array of world-beating onboard sensors, and from net-enabled, off-board sensors, and which present him with a seamless real-time, intuitive, 360o view of the battlespace. This gives unrivalled situational awareness, and this allows him to enter the fight on his own terms.

**"The F-22 has all of these features, conferring a quantum leap in lethality and survivability and making it arguably the world's only true 'fifth generation' fighter."**

*Steven Rainey piloted one of the chase aircraft for the first flight of Raptor 01, and subsequently became the first air force pilot to fly the F-22. He later became commander of the USAF 411th Flight Test Squadron before retiring - only to be hired as one of six civilian test pilots at Edwards. Rainey was then Boeing's lead F-22 test pilot, and eventually Lockheed Martin's chief F-22 test pilot. This was one of the first photos showing the F-22's cockpit. US Air Force, James Haseltine*

> ## "Nor, in an age of 'net centric warfare' does the F-22A have adequate means of contributing its full sensor picture to the rest of the force."

As the range closes, but still above 100nm, the ALR-94 can cue the APG-77 to acquire the target and search for other aircraft in the hostile flight. It does so with such precision that it can use a very narrow beam, as small as 2° in azimuth and elevation – equivalent to what one Lockheed source described as "a laser beam, not a searchlight." The ALR-94 can use a narrowband interleaved search and

## AESA RADAR

The Northrop Grumman APG-77 radar is probably the most advanced AESA radar in service today, with a reported maximum range against a fighter-sized target in excess of 180 nautical miles. This radar incorporates an ultra-high resolution target recognition mode, offering centimetric resolution at extreme range. Returns are matched to an onboard library to facilitate non-co-operative target recognition (NCTR).

The radar's own emissions are carefully and automatically managed, so that signal intensity, duration and space are tailored to maximise pilot situational awareness while minimising any chance of the emissions being intercepted. Targets are carefully prioritised and are subject to greater radar 'attention' as they get closer to the F-22A, first being identified and prioritised, before being continuously tracked, once close enough to be engaged or avoided.

The Sanders ALR-94 passive receiver system is claimed by Lockheed's Tom Burbage, former F-22 programme manager, to be "the most technically complex piece of equipment on the aircraft" and has been described as "the most effective passive system ever installed on a fighter." ALR-94 can detect, track, and identify an enemy fighter radar at ranges of 250nm or more, long before that radar could see the F-22. The system determines the bearing, range, and type of any threat, and then computes the distance at which the threat radar can detect the F-22A.

*This is the cockpit of the F-22A Raptor test aircraft displayed at the National Museum of the US Air Force at Dayton, Ohio. US Air Force*

*The only officially released photo of the F-22 cockpit – actually an avionics rig, probably with unrepresentative symbology. Lockheed Martin*

The AIM-120 AMRAAM is the Raptor's primary weapon for BVR air to air combat, though it is expected to give way to the AIM-260 JATM. A Block 30 F-22 from the 422nd Test and Evaluation Squadron fires an AIM-120 missile over the Gulf of Mexico during a Combat Archer mission on March 18, 2009, flown from Tyndall Air Force Base. The Combat Archer Weapons System Evaluation Program (WSEP) evaluates live air-to-air firing scenarios from end to end. *US Air Force, Technical Sergeant Jason Wilkerson*

track (NBILST) mode to track enemy fighters, with the APG-77 radar being used sparingly to provide the precise range and velocity data to set up a BVR missile engagement. In some circumstances, ALR-94 can provide almost all of the information necessary to launch an AIM-120 AMRAAM and guide it to the target.

The data from the radar, ALR-94 and offboard sensors are correlated into a single track file, with weight given to the most accurate sensor, such that the most accurate range will be from the APG-77, while the passive system may provide the most accurate data in azimuth.

All of this ensures that the F-22A gives its pilots better battlefield situational awareness than has been enjoyed by any other warfighter in history. The aircraft is a key enabler that guarantees air dominance (and not just air superiority) in any threat environment, allowing friendly forces to operate safely and effectively even in the face of the most sophisticated enemy threat environment, and to do so from day one of a conflict.

## AIR DOMINANCE

This is perhaps just as well, as today's US forces have to 'win big'. Narrow victories are not enough. General John M. Loh, a former head of Tactical Air Command, noted that the expectation now was that the USA would "win quickly, decisively, with overwhelming advantage, and with few casualties. Congress and the public now expect US forces to prevail by 99-1, not by 55-54 in double overtime."

General Charles A. Boyd, former deputy commander in chief of US European Command observed that a single question was fundamental: "How many casualties is this nation really willing to absorb? My own feeling is, very few...I think their toleration of casualties is very, very low."

What this means for US air power is that mere air superiority is no longer enough, and that instead, air dominance must be achieved.

Today, the US Air Force defines a 'scale of air power', ranging from air denial, through air superiority, and on to air supremacy and finally air dominance. Air denial is that state in which friendly aircraft can conduct air operations sufficient to deny the enemy air dominance while conducting those airpower activities necessary to halt an initial enemy advance. Air superiority may be defined as the ability to conduct operations without prohibitive interference by the opposing force. Air supremacy goes further, describing the state in which the opposing air force is incapable of effective interference. Air dominance exists where enemy air power cannot operate at all, and where all friendly bombs hit enemy targets while no enemy bombs hit friendly targets, allowing the war to be won quickly (as occurred in the Six-Day War in 1967 and in Operation Desert Storm in 1991), with few friendly casualties.

## HIGH COST

But for all of its considerable potential, the F-22A has been dogged by controversy, and

The first supersonic AIM-9X Sidewinder air-to-air missile launch from an F-22 Raptor (EMD aircraft 4006) was carried out on July 30, 2012, over the Point Mugu Test Range, with Major Howland Ryan at the controls. The first launch of an AIM-9X from the F-22 was carried out in May, 2012. *Lockheed Martin*

the aircraft's very high cost has seen the programme cut back again and again. The United States Air Force originally planned to order 750 Advanced Tactical Fighters (as the F-22 was then known), but this total was reduced to 648 in 1990, and then to 442, with subsequent reductions taking the total to 442, 339, 227, and finally, in 2006, to just 183 aircraft. A subsequent revision saw this increased to 187 F-22As. The USAF retains a requirement for as many as 381 Raptors and has made recent efforts to increase the total to 243, without success. $28bn has already been 'sunk' in the Raptor's research, development and testing, and procurement of the type cost a further $34bn, bringing the total to $62bn, and giving a unit cost of $339m per aircraft. The incremental unit cost of one additional F-22 has been calculated to be around $138m!

The aircraft has also suffered some technical teething problems since it attained its Initial Operational Capability (IOC) on December 15, 2005, and these undoubtedly constrained the type's initial operational usefulness, even after the type was declared fully operational on December 12, 2007. But most of these problems have now been solved, as recently retired Lieutenant Colonel Lansing Pilch, CO of Langley's 27th Fighter Squadron, recently told *Air Forces Monthly* magazine. "The problems we had with software, avionics, sensor tasking and sensor fusion back in 2003 when I joined the F-22 programme have all been ironed out, and we're transitioning to a great point in the next six months where the aircraft will truly be cost effective and fully mature."

Much remains to be done, of course. The F-22A still lacks a helmet mounted sighting system for off-boresight weapons aiming (thanks to technical difficulties in 'mapping' the Raptor's cockpit), and the AIM-9X missile has yet to be integrated. Nor, in an age of 'net centric warfare' does the F-22A have adequate means of contributing its full sensor

The GPS-guided JDAM was the F-22's first air-to-ground weapon. Lt Col Wade Tolliver, director of operations for the 27th Fighter Squadron, at Langley Air Force Base, Virginia, releases a 1,000lb GBU-32 Joint Direct Attack Munition (JDAM) over the Utah Test and Training Range, at Hill Air Force Base, on October 20, 2005, during the Combat Hammer Air-to-Ground Weapons System Evaluation Programme. *US Air Force, Master Sergeant Michael Ammons*

picture to the rest of the force. The aircraft has an excellent intra-flight data link that allows F-22As to share data almost seamlessly, but work is still underway to allow the aircraft to transfer data off-board to legacy fourth generation aircraft such as the F-15 or F-16 (and to Command and Control platforms) other than by means of voice communications, which are slow and inefficient.

Nor does the F-22A have much more than a niche air-to-ground capability, and indeed it was the lack of what Defense Secretary Robert Gates called "sufficient multi-mission capability for current military operations" that resulted in the Obama administration's decision to end F-22 production at just 187 fighters.

The aircraft can, however, carry a pair of bomb racks internally, replacing four of the six medium range missiles in the centre bays, and these racks can each carry one medium-size

bomb (JDAM) or four small diameter bombs each. By carrying bombs internally, the F-22A maintains its stealth capability and retains the ability to supercruise, providing a useful ability to strike targets deep inside enemy territory with precision, little warning, and virtual immunity to enemy defences. Indeed, it is believed that it is this aspect of the Raptor's capability that allowed the USAF to retire the F-117A from the inventory. The F-22A cannot, however, self-designate laser guided weapons, unlike the F-117A or the new F-35A, and this means that it lacks the ability to engage moving targets, or to attack ground targets in a GPS-denied environment.

The Raptor's high speed launch capability can impart significant extra energy to any ordnance dropped, and it has been calculated that a JDAM dropped by a supercruising F-22 might have double the effective range

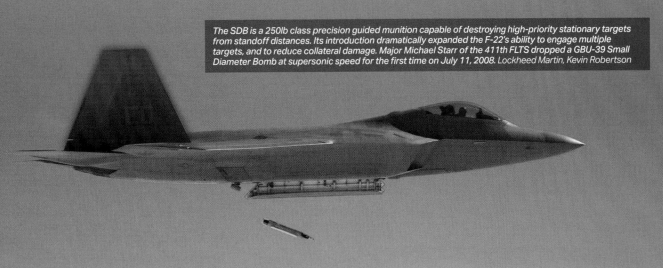

The SDB is a 250lb class precision guided munition capable of destroying high-priority stationary targets from standoff distances. Its introduction dramatically expanded the F-22's ability to engage multiple targets, and to reduce collateral damage. Major Michael Starr of the 411th FLTS dropped a GBU-39 Small Diameter Bomb at supersonic speed for the first time on July 11, 2008. *Lockheed Martin, Kevin Robertson*

*"All of this ensures that the F-22A gives its pilots better battlefield situational awareness than has been enjoyed by any other warfighter in history."*

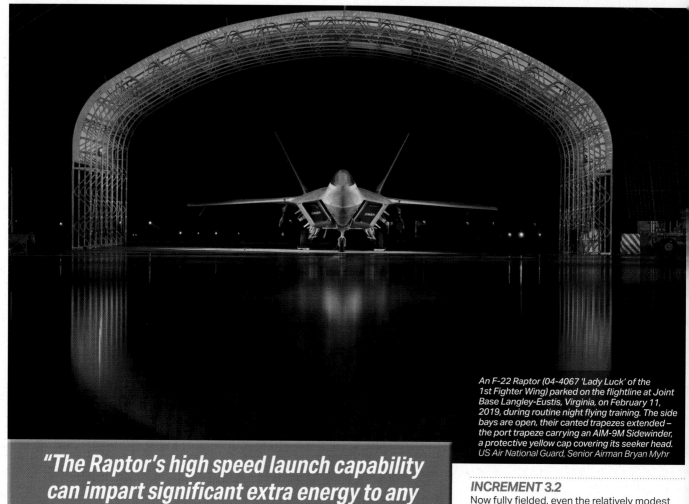

An F-22 Raptor (04-4067 'Lady Luck' of the 1st Fighter Wing) parked on the flightline at Joint Base Langley-Eustis, Virginia, on February 11, 2019, during routine night flying training. The side bays are open, their canted trapezes extended – the port trapeze carrying an AIM-9M Sidewinder, a protective yellow cap covering its seeker head. US Air National Guard, Senior Airman Bryan Myhr

## "The Raptor's high speed launch capability can impart significant extra energy to any ordnance dropped."

compared to munitions dropped by legacy platforms. During tests, a 1,000lb JDAM dropped by an F-22 cruising at Mach 1.5 at 50,000ft hit a moving target at 24 miles range.

Though the F-22A demonstrated its ability to drop JDAMs in June 2006, getting an operational air-to-ground capability took rather longer. Increment 3.1 software, tested in June 2009, provided a basic ground attack capability using Synthetic Aperture Radar mapping, and allowed use of the GBU-39

Small Diameter Bomb. The software for the Increment 3.1 upgrade was not operationally tested on the F-22A until late 2010, however. Some 63 combat-coded Block 30s were fielded with Increment 3.1 software, while the last 83 combat-coded Block 35s (and three test aircraft) were fielded with Increment 3.2, giving an advanced SDB capability. The first 34 Block 20 aircraft, used for test and training, did not have any more than a training air-to-ground capability.

### INCREMENT 3.2
Now fully fielded, even the relatively modest air to ground capability conferred by Increment 3.2, coupled to the F-22's unique combination of advanced stealth, supercruise, manoeuvrability and integrated avionics have made the aircraft a key part of the USAF's 'Day One', 'Kick down the door' force. The F-22 would still play a vital part in winning vital freedom of movement for all follow-on forces.

Nor has the F-22A yet overcome its early reputation as being something of a 'maintenance hog' and it has still failed to meet the USAF's requirement for 12 hours of maintenance per flight hour, or less, requiring 34 maintenance man hours of per flying hour (MMH/FH) according to the Office of the Secretary of Defense and with Lockheed itself admitting to just over 20 MMH/FH during 2009. The aircraft's stealthy coatings and canopy are a particular maintenance burden, and there have been reports of poor interchangeability of components between individual aircraft, with many parts requiring custom hand-fitting. More serious problems included corroding ejection seat rods, which caused a fleet-wide grounding in 2010. More fundamental design problems afflicted early aircraft, with leaky upper fuselage access panels on some aircraft, inadequate strength in the rear fuselage of the first 41 aircraft, and wing root attachment issues on the first 60 jets, while the first 91 aircraft built suffered fatigue problems with the forward fuselage bulkhead. All of these problems have been addressed through modifications and an enhanced inspection regime, but not without significant cost.

The F-22 was not used (or needed) in Iraq or Afghanistan, and indeed had the type been deployed in its current form it could easily

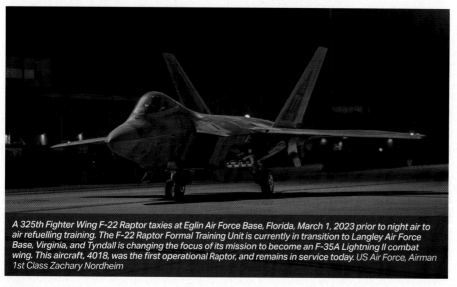

A 325th Fighter Wing F-22 Raptor taxies at Eglin Air Force Base, Florida, March 1, 2023 prior to night air to air refuelling training. The F-22 Raptor Formal Training Unit is currently in transition to Langley Air Force Base, Virginia, and Tyndall is changing the focus of its mission to become an F-35A Lightning II combat wing. This aircraft, 4018, was the first operational Raptor, and remains in service today. US Air Force, Airman 1st Class Zachary Nordheim

Improved connectivity has increasingly allowed the F-22 to operate alongside fourth generation fighters, providing them with greater situational awareness thanks to its enhanced sensor picture, and benefiting from their ability to carry larger numbers of weapons into the fight. Here a 325th Fighter Wing aircraft flies with an F-15E, and F-15C and a Royal Air Force Typhoon. US Air Force, Jim Haseltine

> "The F-22's unique combination of advanced stealth, supercruise, manoeuvrability and integrated avionics have made the aircraft a key part of the USAF's 'Day One', 'Kick down the door' force."

sustainable exchange ratios against 'high end' enemy fighters (developed derivatives of the Su-27 'Flanker', for instance). With growing concerns about Iran, and with the situation in the Korean peninsula deteriorating, the potentially pivotal importance of the Raptor may still be demonstrated in real world conditions.

According to Lieutenant Colonel Pilch, the F-22A offers war winning capabilities in both defence and offense. "Raptor can defend a particular point better than anything else, and we have an unmatched ability to strike hard and deep and with great precision. Finally, we can provide great situational awareness to the rest of the force."

The CENTCOM AOR (Central Command Area of Responsibility) has become a major focus for the F-22 community. An F-22 Raptor (4081) from the 95th Expeditionary Fighter Squadron, based at Al Dhafra Air Base, United Arab Emirates, is seen here flying over Syria on March 5, 2018, during a major surge in activity. The F-22 remains a critical component of the USAF's Global Strike Task Force, able to project air dominance rapidly and at great distances, and to defeat threats if they attempt to deny access to US Air Force, Army, Navy, and Marine Corps force elements. US Air National Guard, Staff Sergeant Colton Elliott

have been more trouble than it would have been worth – lacking key capabilities for those campaigns and being hard to integrate with other assets.

But given an opponent with a robust air defence infrastructure, things would be very different. Only the 'fifth generation' capabilities of the F-22 will give the USA the ability to operate with impunity in a battlespace defended by 'double digit' SAMs, and only the F-22 will provide politically

# The Original 'Lightning II'

## Editor Jon Lake looks at the origins of the Raptor and the USAF's search for a replacement for two already legendary aircraft.

*The rollout of the prototypes was initially scheduled for mid-1989, but ongoing slippages delayed this until November 29, 1990, in the case of the YF-22. US Air Force, Technical Sergeant Bob Simons*

What became the F-22 Raptor originated in Lockheed's submission for the USAF's Advanced Tactical Fighter (ATF) competition. The US Air Force originally outlined an ATF requirement in 1981, looking for a replacement for the F-15 Eagle and F-16 Fighting Falcon, which had then only been in service since January 1976 and August 1978, respectively.

The then classified effort, code-named 'Senior Sky', was spurred by intelligence reports of emerging Soviet air defence aircraft, missiles, and systems, which threatened to erode the USAF's qualitative advantage, and which put the survivability of the F-15 and F-16 in doubt. The new ATF would be expected to be able to survive and operate in what would be a much more contested environment, and to out-fight the latest enemy fighters – especially the Sukhoi Su-27 and Mikoyan MiG-29 fighters which were then known to be under development.

The new ATF was expected to be a next-generation air superiority fighter operating in both the offensive and defensive counter-air (OCA/DCA) roles. Offensive counter-air is the suppression of an enemy's air power, achieved by attacking enemy aircraft in the air and on the ground, and by attacking airfields, related facilities, and aviation infrastructure. Defensive counter-air refers to the protection of one's own territory and forces against attack by enemy aircraft, through defensive combat air patrols, and using ground-based surface-to-air missiles and anti-aircraft artillery.

The USAF Aeronautical Systems Division (ASD) issued an ATF request for information

*Initial ATF studies by Lockheed California, McDonnell Douglas, and Northrop. All would undergo considerable evolution before the final Demval submissions, with canard foreplanes being dropped and canted twin tailfins adopted by all bidders! Lockheed Martin*

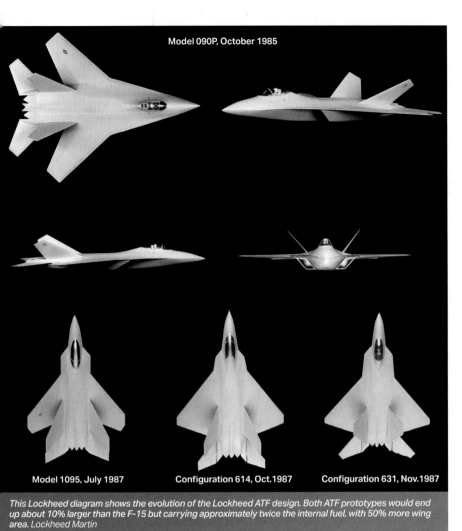

Model 090P, October 1985

Model 1095, July 1987    Configuration 614, Oct.1987    Configuration 631, Nov.1987

*This Lockheed diagram shows the evolution of the Lockheed ATF design. Both ATF prototypes would end up about 10% larger than the F-15 but carrying approximately twice the internal fuel, with 50% more wing area. Lockheed Martin*

manufacturers for further definition of the designs that they had submitted in response to the earlier RFI.

By late 1984, the ATF requirement had evolved and now described a fighter with a maximum take-off weight of 50,000lb (23,000kg), a mission radius of 800 miles (1,300km), a supercruise capability of Mach 1.4–1.5 and the ability to operate from a 2,000ft (610m) runway.

## STEALTH AND SUPERCRUISE

Following a period of concept refinement and definition of the ATF system requirements, in September 1985 the Aeronautical Systems Division issued a demonstration and validation (Dem/Val) request for

> "The new ATF would be expected to be able to survive and operate in what would be a much more contested environment, and to out-fight the latest enemy fighters – especially the Sukhoi Su-27 and Mikoyan MiG-29."

(RFI) to the aerospace industry in May 1981 and then issued a second RFI for the ATF's propulsion systems in June 1981.

A number of design concepts were submitted by the leading US aerospace companies – all of them emphasising stealth, supercruise and STOL, and it rapidly became clear that in order to achieve the required leap in performance, any design would need to take advantage of the latest technologies in fighter design, including stealth, and super-manoeuvrability, as well as the latest composite materials, advanced lightweight alloys, advanced fly by wire flight control systems, and avionics.

It was also clear that the ATF would need more powerful propulsion systems to permit supersonic cruise (or 'supercruise') without recourse to afterburner at speeds of more than Mach 1.5.

ASD subsequently established a concept development team (CDT) to manage concept and technology development. In 1983, the CDT became the ATF System Program Office (SPO) managing the programme from Wright-Patterson Air Force Base.

The USAF Aeronautical Systems Division (ASD) issued a request for proposals (RFP) for the ATF's powerplant in May 1983, as the Joint Advanced Fighter Engine (JAFE). This resulted in the issue of contracts to both Pratt & Whitney and General Electric in September 1983 for the development and production of prototype engines.

In the same month, September 1983, study contracts were awarded to seven airframe

*The YF-22 prototype in final assembly. Unpainted, the aircraft can be seen to make extensive use of composite materials. Lockheed Martin*

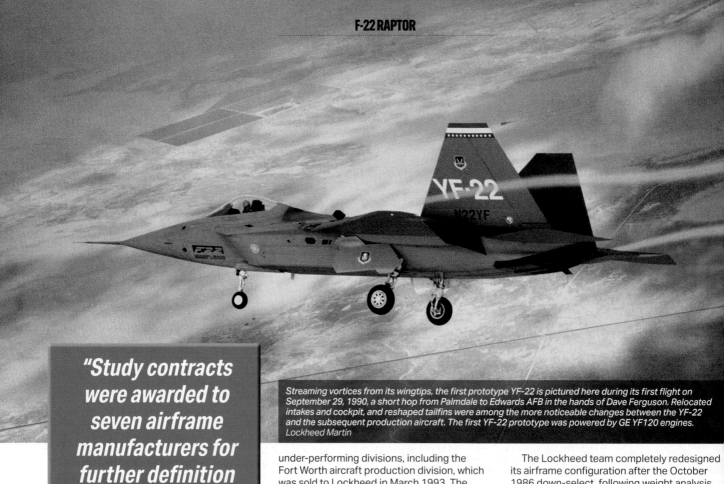

> ## "Study contracts were awarded to seven airframe manufacturers for further definition of the designs that they had submitted in response to the earlier RFI."

proposals. The requirement by now placed an even stronger emphasis on stealth and supercruise capabilities.

The request for proposals would be amended a number of times after its initial release. Stealth requirements were uprated in December 1985, and in May 1986 the RFP was adjusted to include the requirement for flying technology demonstrator prototypes. It was at this time that the US Navy announced that it would adopt an ATF derivative as the basis of its own Navalized Advanced Tactical Fighter (NATF) programme to replace its F-14 Tomcats.

Boeing, General Dynamics, Lockheed, Northrop, and McDonnell Douglas submitted proposals in July 1986, and Lockheed and Northrop were down-selected on October 31, 1986.

With significant investment likely to be required to develop the necessary technology, the companies responding to the RFP were encouraged to band together into teams. Lockheed teamed with Boeing and General Dynamics while Northrop teamed with McDonnell Douglas. Lockheed, General Dynamics, and Boeing agreed to participate in the development jointly if one company's design was selected. Northrop and McDonnell Douglas reached a similar agreement.

The death of Henry Crown, the largest shareholder of General Dynamics, on August 15, 1990, led the company to divest its

under-performing divisions, including the Fort Worth aircraft production division, which was sold to Lockheed in March 1993. The acquisition of General Dynamics gave the renamed Lockheed Martin company control of 67.5% of the ATF programme.

The two selected contractor teams undertook a 50-month demonstration/ validation (Dem/Val) phase, focusing on system engineering, technology development plans, and risk reduction rather than the specific details of the aircraft platform designs.

The technology demonstrator prototypes (Lockheed's YF-22 and Northrop's YF-23) were not intended to perform a competitive flyoff or even to be representative of a production fighter. They did not have to meet every detail of the requirement, but rather had to demonstrate the viability of each team's concept.

The Lockheed team completely redesigned its airframe configuration after the October 1986 down-select, following weight analysis during detailed design. During the summer of 1987, the wing planform was redesigned from a swept trapezoidal wing to diamond-like delta and the planform area of the forebody was reduced, while the number of internal weapons was reduced from eight to six BVRAAMs.

During the Dem/Val phase the contractor teams made extensive use of analytical and empirical methods, including wind-tunnel testing, computational fluid dynamics, and radar cross-section (RCS) calculations and pole testing. The Lockheed team alone conducted nearly 18,000 hours of wind-tunnel testing during Dem/Val. Avionics were extensively tested in ground-based and flying laboratories and rigs.

The contractor teams also conducted performance/cost trade-off studies and

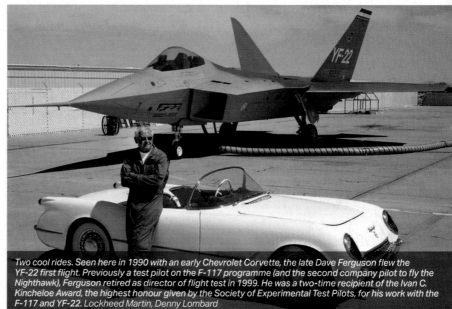

the first YF-22 began on January 13, 1990. The first YF-22 was designated as Prototype Air Vehicle (PAV-1) and registered N22YF. It was later allocated the USAF serial number 87-0700, though this was never worn.

The designs of the two competing teams were not revealed until shortly before the aircraft made their respective first flights. Northrop's first YF-23 prototype was the first to fly on August 27, 1990, and the YF-22 prototype, PAV-1 (N22YF) was unveiled to the public two days later, on August 29, 1990, at the Skunk Works.

The aircraft (powered by GE YF120 engines) made its maiden flight on September 29, piloted by David L. Ferguson. The 18-minute first flight was little more than a short hop to Edwards AFB, during which PAV-1 reached a maximum speed of 250kts and a height of 12,500ft.

## 'LIGHTNING II'

At this stage of the programme, the YF-22 was known unofficially as the 'Lightning II' – named after the Lockheed P-38 Lightning, the company's most successful World War

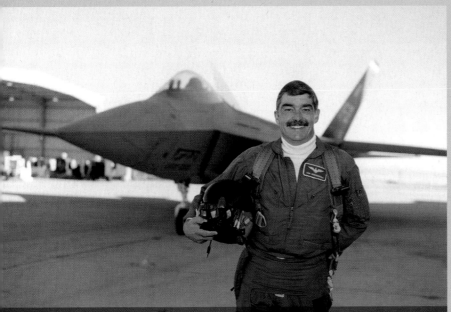

*The Pratt and Whitney YF119 powered second YF-22 made its maiden flight on October 30, 1990, in the hands of Tom Morgenfeld. Morgenfeld joined the Advanced Tactical Fighter programme in 1989 and was primarily responsible for flying the second YF-22A prototype. In 1991 he was named chief test pilot for the Skunk Works and in 1999 was promoted to director of flight operations. Lockheed Martin*

presented them in system requirement reviews (SRRs). This was critical in enabling the USAF to adjust its ATF requirements, deleting those requirements that were predicted to be significant weight and cost drivers, but which had marginal operational value.

One early change was that the initial requirement for an all-new ejection seat was abandoned in favour of using the existing McDonnell Douglas ACES II seat.

The SRRs, coupled with experience from the F-15 S/MTD research aircraft led to a relaxation of the short take-off and landing (STOL) requirement (runway length was increased to 3,000ft from 2,000ft) in late 1987, allowing the deletion of the requirement for thrust-reversers, leveraging a substantial weight saving.

Because avionics were proving to be a significant cost driver, the requirement for side looking radar antenna arrays was deleted, while the requirement for a dedicated infrared search and track (IRST) system was first downgraded from multicolour to single colour and subsequently reduced from being a requirement to being a 'goal'. Space and

cooling provisions were to be retained to allow for these systems to be added back in, if subsequently required.

Despite weight-saving efforts, the gross take-off weight estimate was increased from 50,000 to 60,000lb which in turn drove an increase in required engine thrust from 30,000lb st to 35,000lb st (130 to 160kN).

The final YF-22 design was frozen and the first drawings were formally released in April 1998, and construction of the first of the two YF-22 prototypes began at Fort Worth, Texas, where General Dynamics built the centre fuselage, weapons bays, tail, and landing gear. Each team would build two prototype air vehicles for the Dem/Val phase, one with each of the two engine options - one with General Electric YF120 engines, the other with Pratt & Whitney YF119 engines.

The forward fuselage was produced by Lockheed at Burbank, while the aft section and wings were built by Boeing in Seattle. Final assembly was undertaken by the Lockheed Martin Skunk Works in Palmdale, California, where the major sub-assemblies were shipped by USAF C-5A Galaxy. The final assembly of

> **"With significant investment likely to be required to develop the necessary technology, the companies responding to the RFP were encouraged to band together into teams."**

*The first YF-22 supercruise flight was made by PAV-1 on November 3, 1990. The GE-engined YF-22 achieved Mach 1.58 in supercruise. PAV-2 made its first supercruise flight on November 23, 1990, reaching a maximum supercruise speed of Mach 1.43. Lockheed Martin*

No pilot was allowed to fly both the YF-22 and the YF-23, with the USAF said to be extremely strict but even-handed in the programme. Major Mark Shackelford became the first USAF pilot to fly the YF-22 prototype on October 25, 1990. *Lockheed Martin*

The two YF-22s rarely flew together. On this occasion, the first aircraft can be identified by the spin recovery parachute gantry fitted for high angle of attack trials. Both aircraft were grounded at the end of December 1990, the first aircraft permanently. *Lockheed Martin*

Two fighter. This name persisted until the mid-1990s when the USAF officially named the F-22 as the Raptor. The Lightning II name was then given to the F-35.

Though both teams shared a hangar at Edwards AFB, and both operated under the auspices of the 6511th Test Squadron, the air force very deliberately separated the two teams, who were not allowed to communicate with each other, though the two chief pilots (Ferguson and Northrop's Paul Metz) maintained a channel of communication in case problems with a common system arose (e.g. with the engines), allowing them to communicate in order to maintain and enhance 'safety of flight.' This segregation was such that Northrop's test pilots were kept away from the first flight and were not allowed to observe it. This rigorous separation was relaxed sufficiently to allow a couple of mixed formation flights to be planned and briefed.

Following the first flight, Ferguson said that the remainder of the YF-22 test programme would concentrate on "the manoeuvrability of the aeroplane, both supersonic and subsonic." It was to be a short test programme, lasting only about 90 days. Flight testing continued until December 28, 1990, by which time 74 flights totalling 91.6 flying hours were achieved by the two YF-22 prototypes.

The prototypes were not required to be low observable, although they did incorporate

Tom Morgenfeld used the second YF-22 aircraft to make the first AIM-120A AMRAAM launch over the Pacific Missile Test Range at Point Mugu, California on December 20, 1990, chased by an Edwards F-15D and an F-16D. Lockheed Martin

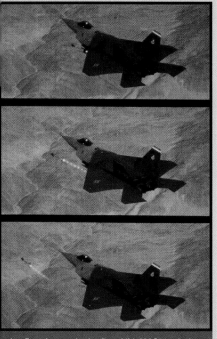

Jon Beesley made the first AIM-9M Sidewinder launch from PAV-2 over the NAWS China Lake ranges on November 28, 1990. Missile firings had not been required under the Demval contract, but Lockheed demonstrated them anyway! Lockheed Martin

Shock diamonds clearly visible, an AIM-120 streaks away from PAV-2 on December 20, 1990. Lockheed Martin

(with P&W engines) becoming the first of the ATFs to achieve this, supercruising at Mach 1.43 on September 18, 1990. The second YF-23 (with GE engines) subsequently reached Mach 1.72 on November 29, 1990.

The first YF-22 supercruise flight was made by PAV-1 on November 3, 1990. The GE-engined YF-22 achieved Mach 1.58 in supercruise. PAV-2 made its first supercruise flight on November 23, 1990, reaching a maximum supercruise speed of Mach 1.43.

PAV-1 made its first thrust-vectoring demonstration on November 15, 1990, and PAV-2 followed on December 1, 1990. With its thrust vectoring nozzles, the YF-22 achieved pitch rates more than double those achieved by the F-16 during low-speed manoeuvring.

YF-22 flight testing did include AIM-9 Sidewinder and AIM-120 AMRAAM missile firings from internal weapon bays, and high angle of attack (AoA, or high-alpha) flights up to 60°, though neither of these was a requirement. PAV-2 made the first AIM-9M Sidewinder launch over the NAWS China Lake ranges on November 28, 1990, with Jon Beesley at the controls. Tom Morgenfeld subsequently used the same aircraft to

"The technology demonstrator prototypes (Lockheed's YF-22 and Northrop's YF-23) were not intended to perform a competitive flyoff or even to be representative of a production fighter."

some radar absorbent materials (RAM) in order to evaluate the durability of these when used on high-speed, supersonic aircraft.

Though a number of USAF pilots were involved in the programme, no pilot was allowed to fly both the YF-22 and the YF-23. Paul Metz later noted that: "The USAF was very keen to avoid a situation whereby a pilot had flown both airplanes and was asked by a reporter 'which is better'? Potentially causing the company to lose the competition. So, the USAF was extremely strict but even-handed in the programme."

Major Mark Shackelford became the first USAF pilot to fly the YF-22 prototype on October 25, 1990.

The second YF-22 (PAV-2, N22YX, later 87-0701) powered by Pratt & Whitney YF119 engines made its maiden flight on October 30 in the hands of Tom Morgenfeld.

All of the ATF aircraft successfully demonstrated supercruise, with the first YF-23

make the first AIM-120A AMRAAM launch over the Pacific Missile Test Range at Point Mugu, California on December 20, 1990. The first YF-22 was fitted with a spin-recovery parachute for these high angle of attack tests (between its 34th and 43rd sorties).

The YF-22 also demonstrated air-to-air refuelling from a KC-135 tanker on October 26, 1990, and the two YF-22 prototypes flew in formation for the first time on December 11, 1990. The first YF-22 ended its flying life when ATF flight testing was suspended on December 28, 1990 having completed 43 sorties totalling 52 hours and 48 minutes.

The second aircraft was also temporarily grounded on December 28, 1990 after completing 31 sorties totalling 38 hours and 48 minutes, having achieved Mach 1.8 on December 26, 1990.

Following the conclusion of flight testing, the contractor teams submitted proposals for ATF production.

*The YF-23 Black Widow leads the first prototype YF-22 Lightning II during a rare formation flight by the two Demval competitors. Lockheed Martin*

The YF-22, with its thrust vectoring nozzles, separate tailplanes, and full-span trailing edge flaperons was judged to be more manoeuvrable than its rival (demonstrating a 100° per second roll rate at 120kts). The YF-22 was also less expensive and was considered to be less risky than the more unconventional YF-23, though the latter was considered to be both stealthier and faster.

Secretary of the USAF Donald Rice announced the Lockheed team and Pratt & Whitney as the winners of the ATF and engine competitions on April 23, 1991, stating that the F-22/F119 combination offered "clearly better capability with lower cost, thereby providing the air force with a true best value."

## NOT CLEAR CUT

The decision was and remains contentious – for both engine and airframe! The advantages were certainly not as clear cut as Rice implied – and the actual reasons for the selection of the F-22

*Major (now Lieutenant General) Mark D. 'Shack' Shackelford, who became the first USAF pilot to fly the YF-22 prototype on October 25, 1990. Shackleford was the US Air Force YF-22A project test pilot on the Advanced Tactical Fighter Combined Test Force, serving with the 6511th Flight Test Squadron, at Edwards AFB, California. Lockheed Martin*

may have been more political than operational. Many believe that Northrop's poor performance on the B-2 Spirit Stealth bomber programme meant that it would face an uphill struggle on the ATF project.

Paul Metz later observed that Lockheed had known how to present and market their airframe far better than Northrop did, leaving 'lasting impressions' through marketing, salesmanship, and sheer pizazz – firing missiles, conducting high Alpha trials, etc.

*One of the two Lightning II prototypes refuelling from a Boeing KC-135 tanker. Despite massive internal fuel tankage, range has proved to be one of the F-22's weaknesses – especially in the Indo Pacific. Lockheed Martin*

He believed that this 'showmanship' heavily impacted the acquisition decision-making process in a way that Northrop's more conservative approach could not.

The press speculated that the Lockheed team's design may have been more adaptable to the US Navy's NATF, providing another tick in another box. Ironically, by fiscal year (FY) 1992, the navy had abandoned its NATF programme.

The Lockheed team was finally awarded a contract to develop and build the Advanced Tactical Fighter in August 1991.

The YF-22s had completed their intended function, and the first aircraft was disassembled and taken to Marietta, Georgia aboard a C-5 where it was used primarily as an engineering mock-up. The aircraft subsequently went to the National Museum of the United States Air Force, at Wright Field, at Dayton, Ohio in May 1997, and was restored for display by March 1998. The aircraft was moved to the Research & Development hangar at the USAF Museum on January 16, 2008, and entered the National Museum of the United States Air Force Loan Program in 2009, being shipped to Edwards AFB on September 2, 2009 on board a C-5 Galaxy, where it was placed on display with the Air Force Flight Test Center Museum.

While PAV-1 was retired from flying duties, the Pratt & Whitney-powered YF-22 PAV-2 resumed test flying on October 30, 1991, for a second phase of testing, to support additional handling tests and some pre-engineering, manufacturing, and demonstration (EMD) work. For these, the aircraft was marked as 87-0701.

The second YF-22 was rebuilt after its accident and was displayed at the Nellis AFB air show from April 24-27, 1997 wearing the spurious serial number 86-022, an equally fictitious WA tail code, and black and yellow fin-tip checkers. *US Air Force*

The aircraft had been taken by road to Palmdale in mid-1991 where it had been fitted with strain gauges for what was planned to be a further 100-hour test programme gathering data on aerodynamic loads, flight control aerodynamic effects, vibration/acoustic fatigue and maximum coefficient of lift while being flown by the 6511th Test Squadron (F-22 Combined Test Force).

The aircraft amassed another 61.6 flying hours during 39 flights until, on April 25, 1992, the pilot experienced a series of pilot-induced pitch oscillations during a touch and go landing at roughly 40ft above the runway. The aircraft hit the runway with the landing gear retracted, sliding some 8,000ft in a shower of sparks before coming to a halt. The resulting fire was quickly extinguished, and the pilot was unharmed. The aircraft was repaired but never flew again, and instead served as a static test vehicle initially for antenna testing at the Rome Laboratory (later part of the Air Force Research Laboratory) at Griffiss AFB in New York.

The aircraft appeared at the Nellis AFB, Nevada air show running between April 24-27, 1997 wearing the spurious serial number 86-022, an equally fictitious WA tail code, and black and yellow fin-tip checkers. Photos of this aircraft often describe it as being the first YF-22 en route to the USAF museum, but Pratt and Whitney logos on the engine nacelles suggest otherwise.

> "Despite weight-saving efforts, the gross take-off weight estimate was increased from 50,000 to 60,000lb which in turn drove an increase in required engine thrust."

The second YF-22 ended up as an antenna testbed, sitting atop a pole at Rome Laboratory (later part of the Air Force Research Laboratory) at Griffiss AFB in New York. *US Air Force*

Raptor 4001, the first F-22 air dominance fighter, made its maiden flight in the hands of former Northrop YF-23 test pilot Paul Metz on September 7, 1997. The aircraft had worn a stars and stripes ribbon and the name Spirit of America when rolled out, but this marking was removed prior to the first flight. US Air Force

# EMD – Birth of the Raptor

The race had been won and the Lockheed Martin/Boeing partnership was charged with taking the USAF's new airframe from concept through to warfighting standards.

The Dem/Val phase was followed by full-scale development, also known as Engineering & Manufacturing Development (EMD). The EMD programme contract was awarded to Lockheed Martin on August 2, 1991, for 11 flying prototypes, plus one static structural loads test article (c/n 3999) and one fatigue test airframe (4000). Some reports suggest that a full-scale RCS pole model (3998) was also included in the EMD contract.

While Lockheed had primarily performed Dem/Val work at its Skunk Works sites in Burbank and Palmdale, California, it moved its programme office from Burbank to Marietta, Georgia, for EMD work. Final assembly remained at Marietta. F-22 programme partner Boeing provided additional airframe components as well as avionics integration and training systems, primarily from its facilities in Seattle, Washington.

Though the production F-22 design had a similar configuration to the YF-22 demonstrator, the aircraft was extensively redesigned, not least to ensure a service life of 8,000 hours, and to balance low observable characteristics with both performance and supportability and maintainability. Weight growth during EMD caused a slight reduction in projected range and in manoeuvrability.

However, the aircraft's redesign also improved overall aerodynamics, structural strength, and stealth characteristics.

In plan view, the engine intakes were moved aft by about 14in, while the wing leading edge sweep was reduced from 48° to 42°, effectively moving the wing aft, while the rear

> ### The aircraft's redesign also improved overall aerodynamics, structural strength, and stealth characteristics."

Paul Metz with Raptor 4002, the latter with a spin recovery chute gantry fitted. For the first flight of 4001, Metz wore his lucky Super Chicken T-shirt under his flying suit. US Air Force

part of each wingtip was clipped to house new antennas. The trailing edge control surfaces were redesigned, and the horizontal stabilators were also redesigned with their leading edges and trailing edges better aligned with those of the wing.

To improve pilot visibility and aerodynamics, the canopy was moved forward seven inches, while the vertical stabilisers were shifted rearward and decreased in area by 20%. The radome shape was also changed for better radar performance.

## CAREFREE ABANDON

Under the skin, perhaps the biggest change was to the F-22's flying qualities, which were considerably refined. The team wanted to make the actual piloting of the Raptor so straightforward that it became a secondary task, freeing the pilot to concentrate on 'fighting' the aircraft. Paul Metz, who had by then jumped horses from Northrop, and was nominated to be the F-22 chief test pilot, explained: "That meant that we put a lot of emphasis on the design of the engine and

the airframe to be tolerant to do anything the pilot can do, we called it 'carefree abandon'. The idea was that you can do anything with the stick and throttle and the airplane will not be harmed nor will it do anything untoward. It won't depart controlled flight or do anything unexpected. That required some

> "Under the skin, perhaps the biggest change was to the F-22's flying qualities, which were considerably refined."

real refinements in the flight controls and in particular the engine logic."

The F-22A preliminary Design Review was completed on April 30, 1993,

Shortly thereafter, in May 1993, the USAF added a requirement for an air-to-ground capability using precision-guided munitions (PGMs). Fortunately, this did not require a further major redesign, though under a $6.5m contract addition issued in May 1993, the main weapons bay and associated avionics were to be adapted to allow the carriage of two 1,000lb GBU-32 Joint Direct Attack Munitions (JDAMs) in place of two of the six AIM-120s.

The addition of this ground attack capability would later result in a short-lived redesignation of the aircraft as the F/A-22. This change was announced by General John Jumper, the then-USAF chief of staff, on September 17, 2002. The designation would revert to F-22A in December 2005.

The Critical Design Review (CDR) followed in February 1995 when Configuration 645 was finalised. This, and an Initial Production Readiness Review (IPRR) of the F119 engine

Raptor 4001 flying with an F-16D chase aircraft. 4001 was shipped to Edwards AFB aboard a C-5 Galaxy in February 1998, where it resumed flight testing in May. US Air Force

The second EMD F-22 refuels from a Boeing NKC-135E Stratotanker while the pilot of 4001 looks on. Nine EMD aircraft flew 3,496 flights and 7,616 test hours during the F-22's engineering and manufacturing development phase. US Air Force

> "The main weapons bay and associated avionics were to be adapted to allow the carriage of two 1,000lb GBU-32 Joint Direct Attack Munitions (JDAMs) in place of two of the six AIM-120s."

allowed the programme to move to assembly of the initial EMD aircraft. The first three EMD aircraft were to be dedicated to airframe, engine, and weapons release testing.

Fabrication of the first component for first EMD aircraft (c/n 4001) began on December 8, 1993 at Boeing's facility in Kent, Washington; while manufacture of the first forward fuselage began at Marietta on November 2, 1995. By now, Lockheed had become Lockheed Martin, following the 1995 merger with Martin Marietta). Fort Worth began assembly work in the Summer of 1995. The mating of the three sub-assemblies that formed the mid-fuselage of first EMD aircraft took place in spring 1996, and the section was then transferred by road

Raptor 4002 fires an AIM-9 Sidewinder air-to-air missile during a separation test at 40,000ft on December 13, 2002. Flown at a 26o angle-of-attack at only Mach 0.4, the test demonstrated the Raptor's ability to operate at slow speeds in a combat environment. 91-4002, nicknamed 'Old Reliable' retired from flight test duties in 2006, and was then used for ground instructional training at Tyndall. It was retired to the Hill Aerospace Museum in December 2022. US Air Force, Justin Brohmer

*During a test mission on July 25, 2002, this F-22 (4003) became the first Raptor to fire an air-to-air missile at supersonic speed, launching an AIM-9L Sidewinder. The aircraft is now on display at the National Museum of the United States Air Force.* US Air Force

transfer to Marietta in August 1996 for start of final assembly.

The number of flying EMD aircraft was subsequently reduced to nine (4001-4009 inclusive), probably when the two-seat F-22B was dropped on cost grounds in 1996. This was not a serious setback, as the USAF felt that the 'carefree handling' of the F-22A, coupled with the use of advanced simulators, meant that there was no need for a two-seat trainer.

Budgetary constraints delayed the F-22 programme, and the planned first flight date slipped back from 1995 to May 1997. The first EMD Raptor (4001) was rolled out on April 9, 1997, when the type was officially christened Raptor. It could have been different – the YF-22 prototypes had been known as the Lightning II, while the name SuperStar had been briefly considered and rejected in 1991.

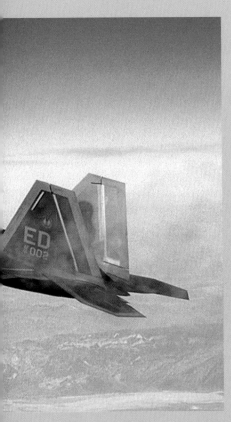

### FIRST FLIGHT
Fuel leaks and hardware-related anomalies led to a further slip in the first flight date to September 7, 1997 and, since Marietta, Georgia, was the production centre for the F-22 it was here, at Dobbins AFB, that the first flight took place. The pilot for the maiden flight was Paul Metz, by now the Lockheed Martin chief test pilot for the F-22 – having previously been chief pilot on the rival YF-23, and then a B-2 test pilot.

Preparations for the first flight had begun nine months earlier, culminating in a dress rehearsal orientation session that lasted a week, going through every considerable potential snag or emergency and working out procedures.

Finally, the aircraft took off from Dobbins Air Force Base, accompanied by F-15 and F-16 chase aircraft. Even though the F-22's landing gear was down, the F-16 reportedly had to use afterburner to keep up. Metz climbed to 15,000ft, where he undertook some manoeuvres and reached a maximum speed of about 250kts.

"The airplane was very much like the simulator. After about an hour came the scariest part — landing back at Marietta. There were a couple of thousand people out there and I didn't want to screw it up," Metz later recalled, describing the aircraft as a 'delight to fly.'

The 58 minute first flight was followed by a second sortie of 35 minutes in the hands of Jon Beesley on September 14. The aircraft then underwent minor structural modifications before being placed in structural test fixture for ground load tests and strain gauge calibration.

After these two flights at Marietta, aircraft 4001 was shipped to Edwards AFB aboard a C-5 Galaxy in February 1998, where it resumed flight testing in May. One of the early highlights was making the first inflight refuelling on July 30.

'Ship Two' (4002) made its maiden flight at Marietta on June 29, 1998, before being ferried to Edwards on August 26. Test points continued to be achieved, and on October 13, 1998, Jon Beesley flew the F-22 faster than the speed of sound.

Weight reduction efforts on 4001/4002 had resulted in these two aircraft falling below the required structural strength for some of

> ## "The first EMD aircraft (4001) was retired in 2000, following the discovery of hairline cracks in the first two aircraft, although the second aircraft was repaired and returned to flight test duties."

the more demanding envelope expansion work, which was therefore delayed until aircraft 4003, an instrumented structural test aircraft, was ready. Meanwhile, the first EMD aircraft (4001) was retired in 2000, following the discovery of hairline cracks in the first two aircraft, although the second aircraft was repaired and returned to flight test duties.

Aircraft 4004 and 4005 were used for much of the initial avionics testing, and aircraft 4006 flew in early 2001. A low-rate production decision in August 1998, after the programme had clocked up 183 relatively trouble free hours of flight testing, meant that the nine EMD aircraft would soon be joined by some more production-standard aircraft.

Lockheed Martin had already received a $503m contact for two PRTVs (Production Representative Test Aircraft), and F/A-22A-10s 4010 (USAF serial 99-010), and 4011 (99-0011) delivered in October and November 2002.

Funding of US $195.5m was released in late December 1998 for the advance procurement of six Lot 1 LRIP aircraft, though these became known as Production Representative Test Vehicle II (PRTV II) aircraft for detailed budgetary reasons.

# From IOT&E to Service

Getting the F-22 into service was not a straightforward process. Every new aircraft has its teething problems, and the Raptor was trickier than many. But since introduction, the type has proven more than capable.

**W**ith the flight sciences and developmental test element of the F-22 flight test programme coming to an end, attention turned to operational test and evaluation (OT&E). F/A-22A number 10 (99-4010), the first production representative test vehicle, was formally accepted by the USAF on October 23, 2002. This first production aircraft (00-4012) was delivered to Edwards AFB to serve with the Air Force Operational Test and Evaluation Center to support the Dedicated Initial Operational Test and Evaluation (DIOT&E) phase. The 422nd TES at Nellis received its first aircraft in January 2003.

Lieutenant Colonel James Hecker, commander, 27th Fighter Squadron, delivers the first operational F/A-22A Raptor (03-4042), the first of 26 Raptors for the 27th Fighter Squadron (the USAF's first Raptor squadron), to its permanent home at Langley Air Force Base, on May 12, 2005. *US Air Force, Technical Sergeant Ben Bloker*

Lieutenant Colonel Dave Rose of the 422nd Test and Evaluation Squadron (TES) at Nellis Air Force Base seen flying the first PRTV F/A-22 Raptor (00-4012) after a historic fly-by of the Wright Brothers National Memorial in Kill Devil Hills, North Carolina on May 12, 2005, in formation with an F-15C Eagle flown by Major Robert Garland of the 71st Fighter Squadron from Langley Air Force Base, soon to be home to the first Raptor Wing. *US Air Force*

Poor 'avionics stability' (e.g., reliability) with the onboard computer operating system crashing every three hours on average, led to the start of IOT&E being pushed back from its planned start date of mid-2003, though this problem was quickly resolved, and there was reportedly a dramatic change in the state of the programme in the year leading up to IOT&E. With its technical and manufacturing problems fixed, the F/A-22A was suddenly 'flying high'.

Following the completion of a preliminary assessment, known as OT&E Phase 1, formal IOT&E (Initial Operational Test and Evaluation) began on April 29, 2004 and this was completed in December of that year.

The fact that aircraft had been delivered to the air force, and that IOT&E was undertaken before EMD had finished, led to fears that concurrency could be a major developmental risk. The number of aircraft at risk (those delivered before development was finished) was small, and concurrency in the F-22 paled into insignificance beside concurrency in the F-35 programme, where the overlap between deployment beginning and development ending ran into years, not months, and the number of aircraft affected was in the hundreds, and not the mere tens.

The five-months of IOT&E trials saw six developmental aircraft fly some 188 simulated air combat sorties, prevailing in every engagement, usually against much larger numbers of adversaries. The F-22 exceeded the demanding requirement that it should be at least 'twice as effective' as the F-15C. Most of the IOT&E pilots were drawn from the F-15C community, and they were united in their enthusiasm for the F-22, which was judged to mark a huge leap over the Eagle in the air-to-air role, which is all that was evaluated at that time. Though the F/A-22's low observable coatings proved much less maintenance intensive than those of the older F-117A and B-2A, IOT&E did reveal that the aircraft required more maintenance than had been expected.

A Follow-On OT&E (FOT&E) test period in 2005 cleared the F-22's air-to-ground mission capability.

In late 2004, initial production of the F/A-22 reached a rate of 18 fighters per year, with the rate planned to increase to 24 per year in 2005 and the maximum 32 per year in 2006. By this time, F/A-22A costs were falling, heading towards a unit flyaway cost of less than $100m (in 2005 US dollars) from the 2004 price of $133m, a 25% reduction.

But in the very month that IOT&E reached its highly successful conclusion, Secretary of Defense Donald H. Rumsfeld directed the air force to halt the F-22 programme at 180 aircraft — 97 fewer than had previously been approved and budgeted for, and 201 fewer than the USAF wanted in order to equip all ten of its air and space expeditionary forces with a single F/A-22 squadron each. Rumsfeld rejected a US Air Force request to spare the F/A-22 and instead cut some of the less-capable F-35 Joint Strike Fighters that were on order.

Air Force Chief of Staff General Teed Michael 'Buzz' Moseley and Secretary of the Air Force Michael Wynne were passionate advocates for the F/A-22 but were unable to save it. Incoming Defense Secretary William Gates, who took

> ## "With its technical and manufacturing problems fixed, the F/A-22A was suddenly 'flying high'."

Guard and Reserve units operate the Raptor, too! Here the Virginia ANG's 192nd Fighter Wing 'flagship' F-22A Raptor is parked outside an 'assumption of command' ceremony at Joint Base Langley-Eustis, Virginia, on Sunday, November 19, 2017. *US Air National Guard, Senior Airman Bryan Myhr*

*The first major change to the Raptor force came with the removal of the type from the 49th Wing, its aircraft being redistributed to other units. The last four F-22 Raptors arrived at Tyndall from Holloman on April 8, 2014, completing the stand up of the 95th Fighter Squadron and giving Tyndall AFB the USAF's largest contingent of F-22As. US Air Force, Airman 1st Class Sergio A. Gamboa*

office on December 18, 2006, was convinced that the air force was not doing enough to support the troops in the field during the counter insurgency campaigns the US was then fighting. He was unconvinced that peer level warfare was a realistic prospect and determined to kill off any further Raptor production.

By the time the EMD phase was concluded on December 27, 2005, Raptors had been delivered to Edwards and Nellis, while the FTU, the 43rd Fighter Squadron, (part of the 325th Fighter Wing at Tyndall AFB, Florida),

had received its first F/A-22A (01-4018) on September 26, 2003. The 1st Fighter Wing's 27th FS at Langley AFB (the first combat-coded F/A-22A unit) had received its first aircraft (03-4042) on May 12, 2005. The type reached initial operational capability with the squadron on December 15, 2005, just under two weeks before the end of EMD!

The 1st Fighter Wing subsequently re-equipped its 94th Fighter Squadron from March 2006, and Air National Guard (ANG) F-22 operations began at Langley in October 2007,

when the Virginia ANG's 192nd FW formally transitioned to the Raptor and relocated to Langley.

The Raptor achieved full operational capability (FOC) with the 1st FW in December 2007.

The Pacific Air Forces (PACAF) Raptors were delivered to the 3rd Wing in Alaska from August 2007, equipping the 90th FS, the 525th FS and Air Force Reserve Command's 477th Fighter Group with the 302nd FS.

The 49th Fighter Wing at Holloman AFB, in New Mexico, became the third operational F-22 unit in June 2008. The wing hosted the 7th FS and the 8th FS, as well as the reserve 301st FS.

The Hawaii ANG's 154th Wing received its first F-22s in July 2010, and deliveries were competed in September 2012. The wing's 199th FS was planned to be the last Raptor unit, as the 15th Wing's 19th Fighter Squadron was an associate unit, without aircraft of its own.

There were insufficient aircraft to sustain frontline wings at Langley, Elmendorf, Holloman, and Hickam, and in July 2010, the USAF announced plans for consolidating the Raptor fleet, with Holloman's aircraft being redistributed to the other bases.

The 325th FW at Tyndall gained an operational squadron and was reassigned from Air Education and Training Command to Air Combat Command in October 2012, though Holloman's 7th FS did not complete the move to Tyndall to become the 95th FS until January 2014.

Lockheed Martin completed the F-22 programme of record when it delivered the final production F-22A (10-4195) to Joint Base Elmendorf-Richardson, on May 5, 2012.

*The next major reorganisation of the Raptor force came in 2018, following the disruption of Hurricane Michael. This forced a move of the Formal Training Unit's flying operation from Tyndall to Eglin, while the other Tyndall F-22 units lost their aircraft to other bases. US Air Force*

A further reconsolidation of the Raptor force followed Hurricane Michael's devastation of Tyndall AFB. This led to the disbandment of Tyndall's 'gun' squadron, and the eventual stand up of a new FTU at Langley, such that the frontline F-22 force is now divided between Langley, Elmendorf, and Hickam, with four full time active duty squadrons, and three National Guard, Reserve, and active duty associate units, as well as the FTU.

## DEPLOYMENTS

The F-22 was originally intended to be expeditionary. The US Air Force structured its requirement for 381 Raptors on the basis of needing ten, 24-aircraft expeditionary squadrons with the extra aircraft for training, test and evaluation, and weapons school work. The number was set at ten such squadrons on the basis that there would be one each for ten standing expeditionary air forces, as part of a mix of integrated fighter, bomber, and support aircraft and personnel that could be deployed on a rotational basis to meet the operational needs of the warfighting commanders-in-chief. Despite a dramatically pruned procurement, F-22s have been regularly deployed overseas.

Over the years, there have been many Raptor deployments to the Indo-Pacific region, to promote regional security, and, initially to deter North Korean aggression, and

*A US Air Force F-22 Raptor assigned to the 1st Fighter Wing prepares to take off at Joint Base Langley-Eustis, Virginia, on November 3, 2020, as part of the 94th Fighter Squadron's deployment to Andersen Air Force Base, Guam. The squadron was deployed to conduct missions in the western Pacific with allies and joint partners. US Air Force, Nicholas J. De La Pena*

> "The number of aircraft at risk (those delivered before development was finished) was small, and concurrency in the F-22 paled into insignificance beside concurrency in the F-35 programme."

An F-22 Raptor assigned to the 1st Fighter Wing from Joint Base Langley-Eustis, arrives at Royal Air Force Lakenheath on October 5, 2018. The unit's Raptors went on to train with US allies and partners as a demonstration of US commitment to European regional security. US Air Force, Technical Sergeant Matthew Plew

## "Rumsfeld rejected a US Air Force request to spare the F/A-22 and instead cut some of the less-capable F-35 Joint Strike Fighters that were on order."

later to demonstrate US commitment in the face of Chinese sabre rattling over Taiwan, and dubious claims in the South China Sea. In February 2007, F-22s from the 27th FS conducted the first deployment to Kadena Air Base on the island of Okinawa, Japan.

Deployments to Kadena have been undertaken ever since, while Andersen AFB, Guam and Osan in South Korea have also hosted Raptor deployments in support of Pacific Command's Theatre Support Package arrangements. Since 2017, F-22s have deployed to Australia every couple of years – to Tindal in Australia's Northern Territories for Enhanced Air Co-operation activities in 2017 and 2022, and then to RAAF Base Amberley for Exercise Talisman Sabre in 2019, while the 2023 edition of Talisman Sabre saw the F-22s deploy to Tindal.

The United States Air Force made an unusually large F-22 deployment to the region in July 2021, sending 25 Raptors from the Hawaii Air National Guard and from Joint Base Elmendorf-Richardson, Alaska to Guam for Exercise Pacific Iron 2021.

General Ken Wilsbach, Pacific Air Forces commander, noted that: "We have never had this many Raptors deployed together in the Pacific Air Forces area of operations. The Pacific Air Force is demonstrating that it can deploy as many or more fifth-generation aircraft into the theatre on short notice than (China) currently has in its entire inventory."

In March this year, F-22s deployed to Tinian for the first time as part of an Agile Combat Employment (ACE) exercise, Agile Reaper 23-1.

Raptors have been deploying to the Middle East since 2009, when six 1st FW F-22s participated in Exercise Iron Falcon at the United Arab Emirates Air Warfare Centre at Al Dhafra, though little publicity was allowed.

There were reportedly four separate occasions when F-22s were scheduled to go to a war zone, only to have the deployment cancelled by the chairman of the Joint Chiefs of Staff on orders from Defense Secretary Robert Gates, who preferred to lambast the US Air Force for its supposed failure to support ground troops in Iraq, and the supposed lack of usefulness of the F-22. Gates railed against what he called "the propensity of much of the defence establishment to be in favour of acquiring what might be needed in a future conflict" rather than the tools required for the ongoing war in Iraq.

Retired Lieutenant General David Deptula said that the F-22s: "were supposed to go in 2008 but were cancelled at the last minute."

The initial operational deployment to southwest Asia in support of US Central Command finally began in April 2012 (after Robert Gates had been replaced by Leon Panetta in June 2011). F-22As from the 7th FS were deployed to Al Dhafra Air Base, as part of the based 380th Air Expeditionary

In August 2022, F-22 Raptors from the 90th Fighter Squadron, 3rd Wing, Joint Base Elmendorf-Richardson, Alaska deployed to the 32nd Tactical Air Base, Łask, Poland. They were there to support NATO Air Shielding, operating as the 90th Expeditionary Fighter Squadron. US Air Force, Staff Sergeant Danielle Sukhlall

Wing. Thereafter, each combat-coded F-22A squadron deployed to Al Dhafra in turn.

During one such deployment, in March 2013, a pair of F-22As, conducting a high value air asset escort (HVAAE) mission, intercepted an F-4 Phantom belonging to the Islamic Republic of Iran Air Force when it flew too close to an unmanned USAF MQ-1B in international airspace over the Persian Gulf. One F-22 flew below the Phantom, photographing it, and remained undetected by the F-4 until the other Raptor pilot pulled up alongside and made a radio call suggesting that the Iranian pilots "really ought to go home!"

## EUROPE

Had the USAF been allowed to procure its originally planned total of 750 F-22s (or even the reduced total of 648) they would have replaced F-15As and F-15Cs almost one-for-one, and Europe could have been expected to host at least one F-22 wing – and probably two. But with the much reduced total and the end of the Cold War, the F-22 didn't appear in European skies for some years. That all changed after the Russian invasion of Crimea in 2014, which left no doubt as to Russia's resurgent ambitions. Thereafter, bolstering Europe's defences and deterring further Russian expansion became more of a priority, and F-22 deployments to Europe began.

The first such deployment began in August 2015 when four 95th FS F-22s deployed to Spangdahlem Air Base, Germany. In April 2016, the USAF deployed 12 95th Fighter Squadron F-22A Raptors to RAF Lakenheath. From there, two aircraft made a brief ACE deployment to Mihail Kogalniceanu Air Base, in Romania, and two also briefly deployed to Siauliai Air Base in Lithuania. August 8, 2018 saw the same squadron deploy to Spangdahlem Air Base in Germany, forward deploying from Germany to

> **"Over the years, there have been many Raptor deployments to the Indo-Pacific region, to promote regional security, and, initially to deter North Korean aggression."**

operational locations in other NATO nations to maximise training opportunities.

On August 4, 2022, 12 F-22s from the 90th Fighter Squadron, Joint Base Elmendorf-Richardson, Alaska deployed to the 32nd Tactical Air Base at Łask in Poland, to support the NATO air shielding mission. In October 2022, four of these aircraft deployed to Leeuwarden Air Base, marking the first time that the F-22 Raptor had deployed to the Netherlands.

Since then, Langley's 94th Expeditionary Fighter Squadron deployed 12 F-22 Raptors to Poland's Powidz Air Base in April 2023, from where a handful of aircraft executed an Agile Combat Employment deployment to Ämari Air Base, Estonia, on May 8, 2023.

## RAPTOR AT WAR

The F-22 was expensive to operate and costly and difficult to maintain, while the USAF was also paranoid about maintaining secrecy. These factors mitigated against deploying it 'forward' into operational theatres, where maintaining its 'stealth' coatings would have been problematic, and exposing its

real world RCS and signatures would have been undesirable. And in the asymmetric, counterinsurgency wars that dominated the post 9/11 world, there was little actual need to do so. The F-22 was, at its heart, an air dominance fighter with a limited and niche air to ground capability best employed in highly contested environments – which were not to be encountered over Iraq or Afghanistan, and where enemy combat air capabilities were conspicuously absent.

But in Syria, circumstances were different, since the regime of Bashar al-Assad had bolstered its air force and air defences with aid and support from Russia, and these remained 'formidable'. President Barack Obama authorised the use of military force against the so-called Islamic State (IS) in early August 2014, initially in Iraq, but subsequently in Syria.

The Raptor's combat debut occurred on the night of September 22/23, 2014, when the United States and its allies (including Jordan, Saudi Arabia, Bahrain, Qatar, and the United Arab Emirates) carried out 14 airstrikes against IS targets in Syria, the first time that strikes had been launched against IS in Syria.

Four Raptors from the 1st FW's 27th Fighter Squadron deployed to Al Dhafra forming part of a strike package that also included F-15Es, F-16s, F/A-18s, and B-1B bombers. Although the Raptors had been deployed to Al Dhafra Air Base in the United Arab Emirates, those involved in the first wave of air strikes reportedly took off from Al Udeid Air Base in Qatar, alongside the KC-10 Extenders that refuelled them.

The air strikes followed a first wave of attacks using TLAM cruise missiles, which struck IS targets around Aleppo, Syria. The USAF package attacked 22 target sets including headquarters, training camps, barracks, and combat vehicles, employing some 200 weapons.

The F-22s attacked an IS command-and-control facility in Raqqah in northern Syria, about 75 miles from the Turkish border. The aircraft used GPS-guided 1,000lb GBU-32 Joint Direct Attack Munitions (JDAMs) to target the facility.

For the attack, the F-22s refuelled from a KC-10 before accelerating to Mach 1.5,

An F-22 Raptor from the 95th Fighter Squadron, Tyndall Air Force Base, taxiing at Spangdahlem Air Base, Germany on August 29, 2018. The Raptor had been deployed to Europe as a part of the European Deterrence Initiative. US Air Force, Airman 1st Class Valerie Seelye

Raptors from the 199th Fighter Squadron fly alongside a KC-135 Stratotanker from the 909th Air Refueling Squadron during fifth-generation fighter training near Mount Fuji, Japan, April 1, 2021. The F-22 Raptors operated out of Marine Corps Air Station Iwakuni, Japan, in support of US Indo-Pacific Command's dynamic force employment concept. *US Air Force, Senior Airman Rebeckah Medeiros*

and climbing to 40,000ft to penetrate Syrian airspace, having to pull back on the power to avoid accelerating past Mach 1.5.

The plan was for two Raptors to attack the command and control centre while the second pair provided air cover. All four aircraft were configured the same way and could have switched roles if necessary. The JDAMs hit their targets within five seconds of the desired time-on-target – after a two hour, 1,200 mile transit, and many delays en route!

The first two F-22s quickly left Syrian airspace and rendezvoused with a tanker, while the third and fourth F-22s stayed on station for about an hour, continuing to provide offensive counterair cover for the remaining strikes. As all four Raptors were finally heading home, the AWACS called them to say that the CAOC

> **"There were reportedly four separate occasions when F-22s were scheduled to go to a war zone, only to have the deployment cancelled by the chairman of the Joint Chiefs of Staff on orders from Defense Secretary Robert Gates."**

needed them to escort a B-1B as it reattacked targets that had not been knocked out.

It was quickly determined that only two F-22s were required to escort the B-1B so the third and fourth jets refuelled from a KC-135 tanker near the Iranian border before heading for western Syria with the bomber, providing air cover for the B-1 for another 30-45 minutes before finally refuelling for a third time and heading home.

The 27th Expeditionary Fighter Squadron had been preparing to leave Al Dhafra when called into action, and groundcrews had to reconfigure its aircraft, removing ferry tanks and refitting weapons! Just days after the mission the 95th Expeditionary Fighter Squadron arrived at Al Dhafra to replace the 27th EFS. During the F-22's first full combat deployment that followed, the six Raptors completed 172 combat missions including kinetic strikes, Combat Air Patrol (CAP), strike group escort and HVAAE. These totalled more than 1,000 combat hours and saw the delivery of more than 150 JDAMs. They also provided protection for 967 coalition aircraft that struck more than 1,200 IS targets. The six F-22As returned to Tyndall on April 14, 2015, after making way for the 94th EFS.

The threat picture in Syria changed markedly after Russia responded to a request by the Assad government for military aid against opposition militias and IS in the Syrian civil war from September 2015. Russia's intervention was focused on shoring up the Ba'athist government in Damascus and fighting American-backed Free Syrian militias (those opposed to IS/Daesh and al-Qaeda).

*A 1st Fighter Wing F-22 seen during operations in the CENTCOM area of responsibility. Deploying the Raptor provides unmatched air dominance and sends an unmistakeable signal to potential adversaries. US Air Force*

Vladimir Putin's primary objective was to try to force a US withdrawal of its own advisors and special forces troops and to roll back US influence.

Russia deployed a range of aircraft to Hmeimim airport near the port city of Latakia, protecting the base and Russian forces in-country with three SA-22, and S-400, S-300VM, and Vityaz (S-350E) surface to air and anti-missile systems, and at the end of January 2016, Russia deployed four Su-35S fighters to the Khmeimim base, thereby producing exactly the kind of contested air defence environment that the F-22 was designed to operate within.

On Sunday November 19, 2017, F-22s (operating with B-52Hs and Afghan A-29s), bombed opium production and storage facilities in Taliban-controlled regions of Afghanistan, as part of Operation Jagged Knife. The F-22 was selected because its ability to use the 250lb SDB promised extremely low collateral damage, but it was like using a sledgehammer to crack a nut, and the F-22 was not routinely used in Afghanistan thereafter. It did, however, return to bombing missions in Syria.

F-22s took part in the Battle of Khasham, (also known as the Battle of Conoco Fields), on February 7, 2018, when the US-backed Operation Inherent Resolve coalition mounted air and artillery strikes against Syrian armed forces and pro-government militias after they attacked a US military and Syrian Democratic Forces (SDF) position in the area. When it emerged that Russian Wagner Group mercenaries had been killed in the strikes, US media billed the incident as "the first deadly clash between citizens of Russia and the United States since the Cold War."

During a later deployment in 2018, the 94th EFS completed what the Pentagon called the "first-ever F-22 Raptor combat surge," flying 590 individual sorties, totalling 4,600 flying hours and delivering 4,250lb of ordnance. They conducted offensive counter air missions, deep into Syrian territory that deterred almost 600 Syrian, Iranian, and Russian combat aircraft.

A former commander of one 94th EFS detachment said that the F-22A's advanced sensors and low-observable characteristics allowed the aircraft "to operate much closer to non-coalition surface-to-air missiles and fighter aircraft with little risk of detection," while providing "increased situational awareness for other coalition aircraft while simultaneously delivering precision air-to-ground weapons."

*Two F-22s from JB Pearl Harbor-Hickam, Hawaii, supported by a KC-135 tanker, deployed at short notice to Wake Island for four days in May 2013. The deployment confirmed that Wake Island—some 2,300 miles west of Hawaii—was a viable divert location for Hickam's aircraft in the event of a hurricane or tsunami warning or in scenarios requiring the presence of combat aircraft. US Air Force*

# Raptor Retirement

So, Lockheed Martin's F-22 Raptor, arguably the finest aircraft of its type, is on the way out. But when, and why?

When the US responded to what Lieutenant General Alexus Grynkewich, Ninth Air Force (Air Forces Central) commander, and Combined Forces Air Component Commander for US Central Command called "Russian unprofessional behaviour in the air" over Syria, it was perhaps inevitable that F-22s would be deployed. The situation seemed to be worsening, with more frequent instances of Russian violations of established deconfliction protocols, with armed Russian aircraft engaging in the 'harassment' of US ground forces and attacking US-supported opposition forces. All this was happening in a theatre in which Russia had deployed its best fighter aircraft, and the lethal S-400 surface to air missile system. It was clearly a job for the USAF's best air dominance fighter.

Thus, it was, on or around June 14, 2023, that the USAF deployed Lockheed Martin F-22 Raptors from the 94th Fighter Squadron at Joint Base Langley–Eustis in Virginia to Muwaffaq Salti Air Base in Jordan.

And the deployment was far from being a one-off.

Two months earlier, Joint Base Langley-Eustis' 94th Expeditionary Fighter Squadron had deployed 12 F-22 Raptors to Powidz Air Base in Poland in support of the NATO Allied Air Command's Air Shielding mission along the alliance's eastern flank. And, on May 8, 2023, the squadron executed an Agile Combat Employment deployment to Ämari Air Base in Estonia, to deter aggression in the Baltic Sea region.

By rapidly fielding forces alongside its allies in the Baltic Sea region, USAFE aims to highlight the operational readiness of NATO throughout the European theatre and its ability to respond to defend NATO territory against any aggression. It was clear that this was necessary even before Russia's invasion of Ukraine in 2022, and indeed its earlier

occupation of the Crimea in 2014, with Poland and the Baltic States (the latter formerly part of the USSR) felt to be particularly 'at risk'.

Nor is Russia the only threat being deterred by Raptor deployments. Similar importance is placed by the US on providing stability and security to the Indo-Pacific – not least by deterring China, whose military might is growing apace, and whose activities in the South China Sea threaten regional stability. In March 2023, F-22s from the 525th Fighter Squadron made a weeklong deployment to Tinian, one of the three Northern Mariana Islands. The islands, which are US territory, had never previously hosted a fifth-generation fighter deployment. From Tinian, the Raptors deployed to Clark Air Base in the Philippines, marking another first time US fifth-generation fighter deployment.

Previously, F-22A Raptors from the 3rd Wing at Joint Base Elmendorf-Richardson in Alaska had deployed to Kadena Air Base, Japan, on November 4, to bolster Pacific Air Forces fighter strength as the F-15C started its withdrawal from the base.

*At least four 94th Fighter Squadron F-22A Raptors (including 08-4171 and, seen here, 09-4179 and) deployed to Muwaffaq Salti AB in Jordan (described simply as "US Central Command's area of responsibility") in June 2023 as part of a multifaceted show of US support and capability in the wake of increasingly intrusive behaviour by Russian aircraft in the region. US Air Force, Staff Sergeant Chris Sommers*

Two US Air Force Raptors from the 95th Fighter Squadron flying high over the Baltic, on September 4, 2015. The US Air Force deployed four F-22 Raptors, one C-17 Globemaster III, approximately 60 airmen and associated equipment to Spangdahlem Air Base, Germany from where the aircraft forward deployed to Estonia. US Air Force, Technical Sergeant Jason Robertson/Released

The F-22 has a unique and devastating combination of agility, supercruise performance, low observability, and situational awareness, combined with an arsenal of lethal long-range air-to-air and air-to-ground weaponry. All of this makes it capable of penetrating, operating within and dominating even the most heavily contested airspace, amid hostile SAM engagement zones and enemy fighters, in a way that other USAF fighters simply cannot. This makes it very much the aircraft of choice when top level air dominance capabilities are required operationally – or indeed for maximum deterrent effect.

But back in Washington DC, senior USAF officers were arguing the case for being allowed to retire 32 of its older Block 20 F-22s, leaving only about 149 later Block 30/35 aircraft in service.

In its fiscal year 2023 budget request, the air force proposed retirement of 33 of its 37 remaining Block 20 F-22s – or nearly 20% of the Raptor Fleet. It was blocked from doing so, but the USAF is again proposing divesting 32 Block 20 F-22s in its 2024 budget.

In testimony before the House Armed Services Committee's tactical aviation panel on March 29, 2023, Lieutenant General Richard G. Moore Jnr, vice chief of staff for plans and programmes said that the Block 20 F-22s were not competitive with the latest Chinese J-20 stealth fighters. Speaking at a panel hosted by the Mitchell Institute for Aerospace Studies, Moore added that the Block 20s were "not combat representative." During the same event Moore averred that: "They will never be a part of the combat force. They don't have the most modern communications. They don't shoot the most modern weapons. They don't have the most modern electronic warfare capabilities. They will not become combat representative aircraft, and so we elected to maintain our position from [fiscal year] '23 that it's time to move on from the Block 20."

And while the Block 20 aircraft are currently being used for training, Moore said they are now so out of synch with the frontline Block 35 that pilots have to "unlearn" habits developed

A slightly shabby looking 95th Expeditionary Fighter Squadron F-22 rolls inverted as it departs the tanker somewhere over Syria, during a sortie from Al Dhafra Air Base, United Arab Emirates on March 5, 2018. US Air National Guard, Staff Sergeant Colton Elliott

"By rapidly fielding forces alongside its allies in the Baltic Sea region, USAFE aims to highlight the operational readiness of NATO throughout the European theatre."

*Late block F-22 Raptors (09-4181 and 08-4156) from the 94th Fighter Squadron, lead a pair of F-35A Lightning IIs from the 58th Fighter Squadron, based at Eglin Air Force Base, Florida. The aircraft were conducting an integration training mission over the Eglin Training Range on November 5, 2014. The purpose of the training was to improve integration of fifth-generation assets and tactics. US Air Force, Master Sergeant Shane A. Cuomo*

in the Block 20 before they can become proficient in the combat-coded variant and are effectively receiving "negative training."

Most controversially, Moore alleged that: "Based on the most advanced weapons that an F-22 Block 20 can carry now, it is not competitive with the Shenyang J-20, with the most advanced weapons the Chinese can put on it."

### PARTIAL PICTURE?

All of this presents a somewhat partial picture of the Block 20. The instructor pilots of the 43rd Fighter Squadron (and now the 71st Fighter Squadron) are justly proud of sending pilots to the frontline who are more than merely 'proficient' and would be surprised to hear Gen Moore's characterisation of 'negative training'. Very few US fighter pilots would agree with his pessimistic view of the aircraft's chances against the J-20, which may 'look the part', but whose LO characteristics are limited, and whose operational capabilities are unproven, but which are suspected of being less than those of an F-15EX.

Professor Justin Bronk of the Royal United Services Institute does not rate the J-20. While admitting that the J-20 is "certainly likely to be more capable as an air-superiority platform than anything else the People's Liberation Army Air Force is currently operating," he assessed it as being no match for US or European fourth generation air-superiority fighters "In terms of thrust to weight, manoeuvrability, and high-altitude performance," and dismissed its low observability.

And while the Block 20 F-22 does not compare to the Block 35 in capability terms, it is still a very impressive air dominance platform, and one that will still outperform any

*An F-22 Raptor from the 325th Fighter Wing (actually the wing 'flagship') flies alongside an F-35 Lightning II from the 33rd Fighter Wing over the Emerald Coast. The fifth generation fighter jets flew together in a rare dissimilar formation to salute healthcare workers, first responders and other essential employees during the COVID-19 pandemic on May 15, 2020. US Air Force, 1st Lieutenant Savanah Bray*

The USAF's stealthy B-2 and F-22 are rarely seen together. Here a B-2A Spirit bomber deployed from Whiteman Air Force Base, Missouri, and two F-22 Raptors from the 199th Fighter Squadron (the squadron 'flagship' and 03-4052) at Joint Base Pearl Harbor-Hickam, Hawaii, are seen flying in formation near Diamond Head State Monument, Hawaii, during an interoperability training mission on January 15, 2019. US Air Force, Senior Airman Thomas Barley

"Raptors from the 3rd Wing at Joint Base Elmendorf-Richardson in Alaska had deployed to Kadena Air Base, Japan, to bolster Pacific Air Forces fighter strength as the F-15C started its withdrawal from the base."

other fighter in the US inventory. Going up against the best that the enemy can field, the pilot of a Block 20 F-22 will be more likely to prevail than any F-15EX, F-15C, or F-16 pilot.

Moreover, it would be entirely possible to upgrade these early Raptors to the latest standard, but the USAF has estimated that it would cost $3.5bn to do so, and an additional $3.5bn to continue operating them through to the end of the decade ($485m per year). This is viewed as being cost prohibitive and an unwelcome diversion of resources away from the Next Generation Air Dominance (NGAD) programme. It could also divert manpower and engineering resources away from the F-35 Block 4 effort, and indeed from NGAD. This would be the wrong investment to make, according to Moore, especially in view of the fact that the entire F-22 fleet will be retired in favour of NGAD in 2030-35.

Many have disagreed with the proposal to retire the Block 20 aircraft, and both the House and Senate Armed Services Committees (which oversee funding and oversight of the Pentagon on behalf of Congress), are trying to force the US Air Force to retain and upgrade the 32-33 Block 20 F-22s that it has proposed divesting under its 2023 and 2024 budget proposals.

The Senate Committee called for legislation that would "Prohibit the retirement of F-22 Block 20 aircraft until submission of a detailed written plan for training F-22 aircrew while avoiding any degradation in readiness or reduction in combat capability."

Website *Breaking Defense* reported that the House Armed Services Committee would once again block the air force's bid to retire the Block 20 F-22s, which it described as "a setback for service officials who sought to repurpose the fighter's sustainment dollars to fund its next-generation successor."

An F-22A Raptor assigned to the 27th Fighter Squadron takes off on the first day of Red Flag 16-3, on July 11, 2016. Raptors regularly trounce all comers during exercises like Red Flag. *US Air Force, Airman 1st Class Kevin Tanenbaum*

Two Langley Raptors (08-4155 and 04-4065) fly next to a KC-135 Stratotanker assigned to the 434th Air Refueling Wing at Grissom Air Reserve Base, Indiana, after conducting air-to-air refuelling over the continental United States, on August 21, 2018, during the Northern Lightning 18-2 exercise. *US Air National Guard, Technical Sergeant Mary E. Greenwood*

One such official is air force secretary Frank Kendall, who expressed optimism that the USAF's second attempt to retire the older Block 20 F-22s (a proposal rejected by Congress in fiscal year 2023), stood a much better chance of surviving the round of budget negotiations in FY24.

*Breaking Defense* quoted an aide as saying that the FY23 prohibition on Block 20 divestment still stood and explained that the F-22 proposal is problematic because the Block 20 is combat capable depending on the threat environment; our most advanced F-22, the Block 30/35 aircraft, would then be required to absorb the training pipeline workload, adding unnecessary wear and tear to our most combat-capable fleet and very small fleet of remaining F-22s."

Retiring F-22s at a time when fighters are in such short supply would seem perverse, particularly when the F-22 fleet has always been regarded as being too small, and too over-stretched, and when the aircraft is the most capable air dominance fighter in service.

If the USAF is allowed to retire its Block 20 F-22s, those aircraft will have to be replaced in the test and training roles by a similar number of 'combat-coded' Block 30/35 aircraft. This will significantly reduce the number of Raptors available for operational, frontline duties, and will effectively take the equivalent of more than two squadrons away from the frontline.

A Royal Australian Air Force KC-30A Multi-Role Tanker Transport aircraft refuels a US Air Force F-22 Raptor during trials at Edwards AFB in California. The F-22 and F-35 were cleared as receivers for fuel from the KC-46A Pegasus under a fifth Interim Capability Release (ICR) mission set on February 23, 2022, but the KC-30A is a vastly superior tanker! *Royal Australian Air Force*

"One problem for the F-22 is that there are few really powerful interest groups fighting for it."

A 1st Fighter Wing F-22 pilot completes pre-flight inspections of 08-4161 during night operations at Joint Base Langley-Eustis, on July 11, 2017. Night operations allow pilots to maximise combat readiness in the 1st FW's lines of effort and maintain night navigation proficiency. *US Air Force, Staff Sergeant Carlin Leslie*

At a time when the F-22 fleet is already over-stretched and over-tasked, any reduction in the frontline fleet will harm US readiness and will make it more difficult to fulfil its commitments. The Next Generation Air Dominance fighter that will eventually replace the F-22 is still in the earliest stages of development and remains many years away from being operationally deployed, even if the programme proceeds without any difficulties and delays, which would seem unlikely. If the USAF presses ahead with its plans there will be a growing air dominance gap.

A pilot from the 1st Fighter Wing checks for full and free operation of the flight control surfaces during night operations on July 11, 2017. The slow shutter speed has left a ghostly impression of the control surfaces full deflection! To help increase effectiveness during night operations, the 1st FW has installed new sun shades that incorporate solar powered lights, allowing night time maintenance and flying. *US Air Force, Staff Sergeant Carlin Leslie*

## ALREADY TOO SMALL?

There are already concerns that the USAF's tactical aircraft fleet is too small, at 48 fighter squadrons (and nine attack squadrons) operating around 2,000 aircraft. It can ill afford to lose even a single F-22 squadron, let alone two. The US Air Force's own study of its tactical air requirements is classified, but Kelly has endorsed the conclusions of the 2018 'Air Force We Need' study, which called for a 62 squadron fighter force.

To recapitalise the fighter fleet while reducing the number of types in service, without further eroding overall numbers, is a tough challenge, and one that will require heavy investment, and a steady flow of new aircraft. The air force has calculated that it will need to buy at least 72 new fighters each year if it is to reach the force levels required, with the right capabilities. It is largely failing to meet this target, year on year.

And yet the USAF is now pressing to retire nearly one fifth of its Raptor fleet in the short term, and to retire all of its F-22s in the medium term, as part of its plan to rationalise its fighter fleet from seven aircraft types to four.

The Lockheed Martin F-22 Raptor is certainly the most surprising 'casualty' of the planned reduction to four fighter fleets. The type is still the world's most capable fighter, providing unprecedented air dominance. Before the Raptor, people talked about 'air superiority' – defined as being the ability for

> ## "Only the 'fifth generation' capabilities of the F-22 would give the USA the ability to operate with impunity in a battlespace defended by 'double digit' SAMs."

friendly operations to proceed at a given time and place without prohibitive interference from opposing forces. Air superiority provides freedom of action, freedom from attack, freedom to attack, and freedom of access.

NGAD promises to provide air dominance, and it is widely accepted that it will more than adequately replace the mighty Raptor. Replacing the Raptor with the NGAD is therefore relatively uncontentious, though some have raised an eyebrow at the fact that the fifth generation F-22 will be outlasted by the older and much less capable F-15E and F-16!

Why not keep the Raptor squadrons and divest a portion of the F-16 fleet, they ask – which is a hard question to answer given that the F-22 will always offer greater advantage over the threat than any teen-series fighter could.

There are even some ways in which the F-22 offers advantages over the newer F-35, particularly in the air-to-air role. The F-22 can carry six AIM-120s internally, where the F-35A carries only four, and its sensor suite is better optimised to the air to air role. Moreover, the F-22's superior performance means that it can impart more energy (and thus range) to its weapons and can manoeuvre harder – which can be of pivotal importance in the BVR fight, as well as within visual range (WVR). Though details are highly classified, the

F-22 is usually credited as being 'stealthier' than the F-35, at least in terms of frontal RCS (radar cross section) and probably from the rear-aspect, too. The F-22 is also much closer to being ready to use the new AIM-260 JATM air-to-air missile.

The F-22's small fleet size inevitably contributes to high operating costs and low mission capable rates, and the aircraft has a significantly shorter range than the F-35A, and probably insufficient range for many scenarios now being considered in the Indo-Pacific region. The aircraft is probably less ready to operate with unmanned 'loyal wingmen' than the F-35 is, though in July 2023, an F-22 did fly with a Boeing MQ-28 Ghost Bat autonomous aircraft during Air Force Research Laboratory trials from Edwards Air Force Base, California.

But despite these disadvantages, the Raptor is an unmatched air power asset in both defensive and offensive operations. The F-22 can defend a particular point better than anything else, but also with an unmatched ability to strike hard and deep and with great

precision, and all while providing unmatched situational awareness to the rest of the force.

Only the 'fifth generation' capabilities of the F-22 would give the USA the ability to operate with impunity in a battlespace defended by 'double digit' SAMs, and only the F-22 could provide politically sustainable exchange ratios against 'high end' enemy fighters (developed derivatives of the Su-27 'Flanker', for instance). Plans to cut the F-22 force before its replacement is ready are therefore controversial.

And yet the USAF has put forward proposals to do exactly that.

In 2021, Lieutenant General Clinton S. Hinote, the USAF's deputy chief of staff for strategy, integration, and requirements revealed that the F-22 would begin being phased out in about 2030, though he said that the exact timeline would be situation-dependent. "By about the 2030 timeframe, you're talking about a 40-year-old platform (in the F-22), and it's just not going to be the right tool for the job, especially when we're talking about defending our friends like Taiwan and Japan and the Philippines against a Chinese threat that grows and grows."

## CHINESE STEALTH
He said that the Next-Generation Air Dominance fighter would soon be needed to defeat the Chinese stealth aircraft and missile threat which he characterised as being "closer than we think."

While Hinote acknowledged that the F-22 was a good airframe, and one that had been updated and that will continue to receive upgrades (mostly to its sensors) he said that the F-22 had limitations. "We can't modernise our way out of the air superiority problem just using an updated F-22," he said.

The US Air Force was therefore anticipating "the sunset of the F-22 … in about the 2030-ish timeframe." That would not be the date for the full retirement of the F-22, but the beginning of its phase-out, and Hinote emphasised that the USAF would not allow any gap in its ability to achieve air superiority, which he said was a mission area where gaps or risks would not be tolerated.

*A 154th Aircraft Maintenance Squadron crew chief prepares an F-22 Raptor (05-4098), operated by the 199th and 19th Fighter Squadrons, for a training sortie June 15, 2023, at Joint Base Pearl Harbor-Hickam, Hawaii. US Air National Guard, Master Sergeant Mysti Bicoy*

Major Paul 'Loco' Lopez, the F-22 Demo Team commander and pilot, performs the 'tail slide' manoeuvre in 433rd WPS Raptor 04-4071 during an aerial demonstration at the SkyFest air show in Spokane. Washington on June 22, 2019. Lopez was then in his second year as the commander of the F-22 Raptor Demonstration Team. *US Air Force, 2nd Lieutenant Samuel Eckholm*

wherever it's needed...so the air force has asked us to move forward with that modernisation programme, and then we'll see how long the aircraft endures. There's no limitation on the airplane itself that drives it. That will be a decision in terms of force management and how soon any replacements or other technologies might come along, so we're posturing beyond seven years. We're continuing to think, 'How do we keep the airplane relevant?'"

Brigadier General Dale White, programme executive officer for fighters and advanced aircraft, has acknowledged that the F-22 still needs to be upgraded to address today's threats: "We still have a threat we have to address now. The F-22 represents our ability to address that threat, to be able to be the bridge to NGAD, and in order to do that, we have to keep it modernised. We have to keep it legal and operationally viable."

But these upgrades may not indicate that the F-22 necessarily has a long life ahead of it, as much of the investment is intended to mature technologies and specific systems for the NGAD, and to lay the groundwork for how tomorrow's next-generation aircraft will be supported and sustained. OJ Sanchez has said that: "We're very hopeful that technology development for Raptor will help bridge us to the next set of technologies. Where there are technologies to mature and be beneficial to the Raptor, hopefully those will also find their way into the next generation."

Hinote said that the F-22 would be kept "viable as a bridge to get to the new capability. This is not an area of the air force where we feel we can take a lot of risk."

One problem for the F-22 is that there are few really powerful interest groups fighting for it. It is an inconvenience to its manufacturer, who have no space, manpower, or resources to support it, and other priorities in the shape of the F-35, the Block 70 F-16 and potential work on NGAD. With sky-high support and sustainment costs already, there is no headroom for anyone to 'pad' F-22 support contracts, and little scope for excessive profits. Nor does the aircraft have particular

political cheerleaders. Few jobs now depend on the F-22, so there is little need or incentive for local senators or congressmen to fight for the aircraft – perhaps with the exception of those representing states where the aircraft is based. Nor are there many prominent former Raptor pilots who are active in public life – there is no Martha McSally (the former A-10 pilot turned politician) for the F-22.

But for as long as the F-22 remains in service, with its reputation as the best air dominance fighter in the world, the F-35 will, in some respects, remain in its shadows, and the F-22 will provoke questions as to whether the new NGAD is actually needed. And while the Raptor does remain in service, it will continue to project air dominance, rapidly and at great distances, and will be able to defeat any threats that might attempt to deny access to US and allied force elements.

It will also serve as a pathfinder to the next generation of air dominance, providing a tough and rigorous yardstick, against which the new NGAD will be measured and judged. It will undoubtedly be a hard act to follow.

And should the US Air Force change its mind (or should the NGAD be delayed), Lockheed Martin officials said in August 2023 that the company can and will support the F-22 for as long as the air force wants to fly it, even if that's for a decade longer than is currently planned!

OJ Sanchez, vice president of Lockheed's F-16 and F-22 programs, told the *Defense One* website that military aircraft often stick around longer than expected – citing the F-16, which is still in production today after the after the original line closed in 2018, with a new line established three years later.

Sanchez said that the F-22's future was: "less about how long is it going to be in service and more about the unique capability that it brings to ensure air superiority,

> **"In 2021, Lieutenant General Clinton S. Hinote, the USAF's deputy chief of staff for strategy, integration, and requirements revealed that the F-22 would begin being phased out in about 2030."**

Few would have predicted the F-22 joining the list of America's most endangered fighter aircraft, but like the F-15C it is scheduled for retirement, while the Phantom and F-117 have already disappeared from the frontline. Here an F-22 Raptor, an F-117 Nighthawk, an F-4 Phantom and an F-15 Eagle fly over Holloman Air Force Base, on October 27 during the 2007 Holloman Air and Space Expo. *US Air Force, Staff Sergeant Jason Colbert*

A U.S. Air Force F-22 Raptor sits on the flight line during the Fourth of July firework celebration in Battle Creek, Michigan in 2019. *US Air Force, 2nd Lieutenant Samuel Eckholm*

# F-22 Upgrades
## Blocks and Increments

Two Raptors from Joint Base Elmendorf-Richardson fly in formation over the Joint Pacific Alaska Range Complex, on July 18, 2019. The JPARC is a 67,000 plus square mile area, providing a realistic training environment providing commanders with the opportunity for full spectrum training, ranging from individual skills to complex, large-scale joint engagements. US Air Force, Staff Sergeant James Richardson

**Since its first flight back in 1997, the F-22 Raptor has been constantly assessed, upgraded, and modified. We take a look at this process of evolution.**

Even before the type could enter service, in 2003 the USAF established an F-22 modernisation and improvement programme to add enhanced air-to-ground, information warfare, reconnaissance, and other capabilities, and to improve the reliability and maintainability of the aircraft.

The three technologies that were originally identified as being 'critical' (a 32-bit stores management system, processing memory, and cryptography) were all by then judged as being mature, while three new 'critical' technologies (smaller and more powerful radio frequency components, larger bandwidth, and radio frequency low observable features) were not. By the time the Government Accountability Office (GAO) reviewed the programme in 2007, none of these technologies had been demonstrated in a realistic environment, and were viewed as having demonstrated basic performance,

technical feasibility, and functionality in a laboratory setting, but not necessarily in their planned form and fit (size, weight, materials, etc.).

A disciplined systems engineering process was recognised as having ensured that technologies were developed and matured before being integrated onto the aircraft, though reliability and availability were not meeting required standards.

The US Air Force had originally planned to field enhanced F-22A capabilities in three development increments that were planned to be completed in 2010. Unfortunately, funding constraints (including a $330m reduction in the F-22A's modernisation budget) and changes in requirements and required work content in each increment led to schedule slips, such that the last increment would not be integrated on the F-22A until 2013.

This was In part a result of the need to spend more than had been planned on reliability and maintainability upgrades, and to devote more manpower and effort to

these areas. A key reliability requirement for the F-22A had been a three-hour mean time between maintenance events by the time the programme achieved 100,000 operational flying hours (expected in 2010), and in 2007, the fleet was struggling to achieve a one-hour interval.

### BLOCK 10
The F-22 entered service with Air Combat Command in 2005, taking over the air dominance role from the F-15 Eagle. Although the baseline Block 10 Increment 1 Initial Operational Capability configuration was intended as an air dominance fighter it was at least notionally multirole, with the option of replacing four of six AMRAAMs with a pair of 1,000lb GBU-32 JDAMs (Joint Direct Attack Munitions). This was supposed to provide an analogous deep-strike capability to the F-117A (notwithstanding the inability of the GPS-guided JDAM to engage moving targets, or indeed the lack of a penetrator 'bunker busting' variant) and was said to be more survivable.

An F/A-22 Raptor (00-4015, a PRTV II Block 10 aircraft) taxies at Nellis on July 9, 2007. This was the fourth Raptor to arrive from the factory. Eventually, 17 Raptors were assigned at Nellis. US Air Force, Technical Sergeant Kevin J. Gruenwald

> "In November 2005, the F-22A completed follow-on operational test and evaluation. This evaluated the F-22A's ability to carry out the air-to-ground mission."

In November 2005, the F-22A completed follow-on operational test and evaluation. This evaluated the F-22A's ability to carry out the air-to-ground mission, and also evaluated deferred initial operational test and evaluation items and supported the initial operational capability declaration. The F-22A was assessed as being mission capable and able to complete some limited air-to-ground missions using the JDAM.

## BLOCK 20

Development of the Raptor's Global Strike Basic capability began in 2003, as the first major upgrade developed under the Raptor Enhancement Development and Integration (REDI) contract signed in March 2003. This resulted in the Block 20 (Increment 2.0) configuration, which enabled the Raptor to deliver a pair of GBU-32 JDAMs at supersonic speeds. An improved Advanced Medium-Range Air-to-Air Missile capability was also provided.

The Block 20 configuration was the baseline for the Global Strike Task Force (GSTF) fleet and was originally expected to include

some common radar modules with the JSF, a dedicated high-speed radar processor, and COTS technology CIP processors. The GBU-39/40 Small Diameter Bomb was also once planned to have been introduced in the Block 20 aircraft together with high resolution SAR radar modes, improved radar ECCM, two-way voice and data MIDS/Link-16 capability, improved crew station software, and improved electronic countermeasures. Most of these features were actually integrated later, as part of subsequent Increments.

Follow-on Test and Evaluation (FOT&E) efforts associated with the more limited Increment 2 configuration were completed in August 2007 and deliveries of production Increment 2.0 aircraft began on May 6, 2008, with the formal acceptance of serial 06-4117. Some earlier airframes were later upgraded to this baseline standard.

The project also upgraded the Intra- Flight Data Link (IFDL) enabling

enhanced connectivity between Raptors. The IFDL provides Raptor pilots with an encrypted voice and data communications channel that permits two or more F-22As to automatically share information including target and system data.

Because Increment 3.1 development was not complete, many subsequent production aircraft were initially delivered in Increment 2 configuration.

Under the Common Configuration Program (CCP), the PRTVs and Block 10 and 20 aircraft from LRIP Lots 1, 2 and 3, were all upgraded to a common Block 20 configuration. The CCP provided additional computer memory, faster processors and new power supplies that increased processing capability. All remaining Block 20 models from Lot 1 and Lot 2 have been retained in that Block 20 CCP configuration. Although the Lot 1 and 2 Block 20 fighters could be brought up to the later standards, the service determined that the

Lieutenant Colonel David Rose becomes the first operational air force pilot to fly the F/A-22 at Nellis AFB on January 17, 2003. His mount was 00-4012, the first production aircraft (actually the first aircraft in the PRTV II batch, built to Block 10 standards. US Air Force, Kevin Robertson

*Lieutenant Colonel James Hecker delivered the first operational F/A-22 Raptor (03-4042, the second Block 20 aircraft) to its permanent home at Langley Air Force Base on May 12, 2005. This was the first of 26 Raptors to be delivered to the 27th Fighter Squadron, Hecker's command. US Air Force, Technical Sergeant Ben Bloker*

cost of doing so would be prohibitive and they are relegated to training and support roles.

Most Block 20 aircraft from Lots 3 and 4 have been upgraded to the Block 30/35 configuration.

## BLOCK 30

The Block 30 configuration was originally planned to incorporate side-looking radar arrays and a Satcom terminal to provide continuous network connectivity during deep-strike profiles along with enhancements to provide full 'Wild Weasel' defence suppression and time-critical target engagement capabilities.

Post-2011 there was to have been a Block 40 aircraft. This was intended to be the definitive Global Strike configuration, with full sensor networking, range enhancements, integrated ISR capabilities, and a Helmet Mounted Display similar to that used by the JSF. This was due to be followed by a Block 50 Electronic Attack variant, replacing the EF-111A Raven. The new variant was to be equipped with an LO stores pod for use on the external underwing pylons.

In the event, there never was a Block 50, while both Block 40 and Increment 3 were rather more modest and Increment 3 was split into smaller packages which became Block 30 and Block 35.

Incremental Enhanced Global Strike modernisation efforts included Increment 3.1, which provided the Northrop Grumman AN/APG-77 radar with enhanced air-to-ground mission capability, including the geolocation of selected threat emitters, electronic attack, air-to-ground synthetic aperture radar mapping and designation of surface targets, and integration of the GBU-39/B SDB (Small Diameter Bomb). The Block 30 could carry up to eight 250lb Small Diameter Bombs, replacing four of the six AIM-120s.

Final operational testing and evaluation (FOT&E) of Increment 3.1 began in January

2011 and concluded in November 2011, when it began to be fielded by the 525th FS at Joint Base Elmendorf-Richardson. The 525th subsequently achieved IOC with the upgraded aircraft in 2012.

The 3rd Wing conducted the first large-scale exercise with Increment 3.1 In April 2012, delivering eight live and 12 inert JDAMs against target co-ordinates within the Joint Pacific Alaska Range Complex that had been self-generated using the radars of upgraded aircraft. The 3rd Wing employed SDBs for the first time during a Combat Hammer exercise in early August 2012, this time using the Utah Test and Training Range. This marked the first time

that SDB had been delivered by frontline Raptor pilots, rather than by the test community.

## BLOCK 35

Development of Increment 3.2A began in November 2011. Increment 3.2A was a software-only upgrade providing improved electronic protection and improved communications including a Link 16 Receive mode, and enhanced combat identification capabilities.

Increment 3.2A developmental testing proceeded throughout FY14, with tail number 4007 one of the project workhorses. This aircraft completed its 1,000th sortie on

*Major Paul 'Loco' Lopez about to display at Naval Air Station Oceana in 2018. It is very difficult to tell a Raptor's mod state externally – there are few differences, and many aircraft have been modified and upgraded from one Block standard to another. US Navy*

Airmen refuel two Block 30 Raptors (05-4088 and 04-4079, the latter originally built as a Block 20 aircraft) from the 95th Fighter Squadron, 325th Fighter Wing, at Spangdahlem Air Base, Germany, on August 14, 2018. While the training unit at Tyndall used Block 20 aircraft, the 95th FS used Block 30s. The squadron deployed to Europe to train with other air force aircraft in a realistic environment and reinforce NATO's eastern flank. US Air Force, Airman 1st Class Valerie Seelye

April 19, 2013, during testing of the Increment 3.2A software upgrade package by the F-22 Combined Test Force (CTF) at Edwards AFB, California.

Software stability and radar performance shortfalls were encountered relatively late in the development flight test schedule, requiring additional unplanned software releases in order to demonstrate readiness for FOT&E, which finally began in FY15, having been planned for 3QFY14.

The US Air Force struggled to ensure the availability of the required Air-to-Air Range Infrastructure (AARI) instrumentation system at the Nevada Test and Training Range, leading to further delays.

## INCREMENT 3.2B

Increment 3.2B was a separate Major Defense Acquisition Program modernisation effort that integrated the new AIM-120D and AIM-9X missiles on the F-22, and a Common Weapon Employment Zone for air-to-air missiles, together with an Enhanced Stores Management System (ESMS) to improve weapons integration and employment, enhancements to the Intra-Flight Datalink (IFDL) and electronic protection systems, as well as improved emitter geolocation capability.

The one reported critical technology for Increment 3.2B was a geolocation algorithm, which had been demonstrated in a relevant, but not a realistic environment.

Increment 3.2B EMD efforts began in June 2013 and full technology and design maturity was achieved by the time the Critical Design Review was completed in August 2015. The programme performed iterative software development in a laboratory environment,

before beginning initial flight testing of software.

Nine aircraft were modified to support IOT&E from August 2017 to April 2018. Retrofits to in service aircraft began in May 2019 and a Required Assets Available (RAA) milestone (for six updated F-22As to be operational) was achieved on August 27, 2019.

It was planned for a total of 152 Raptors to receive the hardware and software upgrades – variously described as comprising

> "The IFDL provides Raptor pilots with an encrypted voice and data communications channel that permits two or more F-22As to automatically share information including target and system data."

three developmental test assets and 149 operational aircraft or nine development aircraft and 143 mission aircraft! These 143 airframes consisted of 123 PMAI (Primary Mission Aircraft Inventory) aircraft with six squadrons (plus the Backup Aircraft Inventory (BAI) aircraft assigned to those squadrons. The eight remaining airframes were those assigned to Nellis for the TES or USAF Weapons School.

GAO documents showed that it cost $1.5653bn to bring these 143 F-22As to the Block 30 standard with full Increment 3.2 upgrades (a unit cost of $10.2918 million per airframe).

Block 3.2B upgrades were scheduled for completion by the end of 2021, and Lockheed Martin announced that it had completed 98 of 143 planned Block 3.2B upgrades by May 2021.

## UPDATE 5 AND UPDATE 6

Increment 3 was accompanied by two Operational Flight Program (OFP) upgrades. Update 5 combined an OFP upgrade providing software driven radar enhancements, Automatic Ground Collision Avoidance System software, Intra Flight Data Link Gateway Mode (IFDL GWY Mode) allowing the F-22 to communicate with 4th generation aircraft, and the incorporation of limited Block I AIM-9X missile launch capabilities. The weapons engagement zone (WEZ) symbology in the F-22's HUD was still displayed with AIM-9M characteristics (and not those of the AIM-9X) under Update 5. Full integration of the more capable AIM-9X Block II required the Increment 3.2B upgrades which provided two-way datalink functionality between the F-22 and AIM-9X II, thereby enabling lock-after launch (LOAL) capability.

*Major Philip 'Stonewall' Johnson of the 514th Flight Test Squadron (FLTS) made a functional check flight of 02-4037 at Hill Air Force Base in October 2019, after an extensive seven-year repair of the aircraft at the Ogden Air Logistics Center (OO-ALC). The aircraft had been damaged when it settled back onto the runway during a touch-and-go at Tyndall AFB, Florida on May 31, 2012. US Air Force*

Update 6 represented the next iteration of continuous software improvements for the F-22 and was a software-only OFP effort to update the aircraft KOV-20 cryptographic module with an F-22A cryptographic architecture change to accommodate multiple, simultaneous algorithms for Link 16 datalink interoperability and secure ultrahigh frequency radio communications. Update 6 also included a critical interoperability update and significant improvements to radar and In-Flight Data Link (IFDL) stability, as well as deferred software corrections carried over from Increment 3.2B developmental testing.

The 59th Test and Evaluation Squadron (TES), combined with the 422nd TES and F-22A Developmental Test at Edwards AFB, California, collaborated to fly more than 899 sorties (1,287 hours) on Update 6.

From April 2020, the release and fielding of the F-22 Update 6 Operational Flight Program (OFP) was incorporated into the Increment 3.2B Block 30/35 modification line. This was then expanded to Joint Base Elmendorf-Richardson, Alaska; Joint Base Hickam, Hawaii;

and the Ogden Air Logistics Complex, Utah.

Some 110 of 175 planned Update 6 Operational Fight Program (OFP) software upgrades had been completed by May 2021.

### RACR

The Raptor Agile Capability Release (RACR) capability pipeline is a new programme of iterative updates for the F-22, launched after Lockheed Martin completed the major Increment 3.2B upgrade in 2020-2021, which thereby became the last 'monolithic' major upgrade.

**"Most Block 20 aircraft from Lots 3 and 4 have been upgraded to the Block 30/35 configuration."**

> **"The US Air Force plans to spend $4.2bn in procurement in the fiscal year 2024-2028 period, with another $1.74bn 'to completion', circa 2030, as well as $3.2bn in research, development, test, and evaluation."**

*Though it has an impressive internal fuel capacity, the F-22's inability to carry external fuel tanks without compromising 'stealth' means that it has always been handicapped by range – especially in the Pacific theatre. Here a Langley-based Block 30 refuels from a KC-135 Stratotanker, assigned to the 434th Air Refueling Wing on August 21, 2018. US Air Force, Technical Sergeant Mary E. Greenwood*

The philosophy underpinning RACR is for the F-22's software to be upgraded on an approximately annual cycle, sometimes with accompanying minor internal hardware changes achieved by using rapid prototyping. This, it is hoped, will allow capability to be provided to the warfighter at a significantly faster pace than has been seen in the last decade, with a formal ambition of releasing capabilities to the field on an annual basis.

Achieving this will require 'digital transformation', and the first phase of RACR therefore integrated a new Open Systems Architecture – said to be the first on a US combat aircraft and leading some to describe the F-22 as an example of the US Air Force's Digital Century Series initiative. The Raptor Agile Capability Release (RACR) Release 1 was the first attempt by the Department of Defense and industry to implement agile commercial software practices at scale on a fighter platform. This required what has been the largest hardware upgrade on the F-22 platform in more than a decade, adding a new hardware architecture to facilitate the implementation of the new open systems architecture (OSA).

The F-22A Tactical Link 16 (TACLink) and Tactical Mandates (TACMAN) are hardware and software modernisation efforts which were originally separate programmes, but which have been moved to sit within the

*The final Lockheed Martin F-22 Raptor made its maiden test flight at Marietta on March 14, 2012, with company test pilot, Bret Luedke at the controls. Raptor 10-4195 was subsequently delivered to the 3rd Wing at Joint Base Elmendorf-Richardson, Alaska. Lockheed Martin*

A 27th Fighter Squadron 'Fighting Eagles' F-22A Raptor (03-4058) fires an AIM-120 Advanced Medium Range Air-to-Air Missile (AMRAAM) at a BQM-34P 'Fire-bee' subscale aerial target drone during a Combat Archer mission over the Gulf of Mexico. The unit was deployed to Tyndall AFB, Florida to support the air-to-air weapons system evaluation programme hosted by the 83rd Fighter Weapons Squadron. US Air Force, Master Sergeant Michael Ammons

RAPTOR Agile Capability Release (RACR) Capability Pipeline.

TACLink was intended to provide Link 16 transmit capability via the Multi-functional Information Distribution System/Joint Tactical Radio System and to replace the legacy Mark XVII Mode 4 Identification Friend or Foe (IFF) system with the Mode 5 IFF system.

Prior to the Link-16 upgrade, Raptor pilots used a series of ad-hoc operational procedures to share information with 4th generation fighters over UHF and VHF radio, if no Battlefield Airborne Communications Node (BACN) aircraft were present. Before RACR Release 1, some 72 F-22s received Link-16 transmit capability by 2020. The distribution of

these 72 aircraft among the PMAI squadrons and the exact nature of the Link-16 modification remains unknown, but it may have involved use of the L-3 developed 'Chameleon' waveform to reduce the probability of detection.

Elements of the planned Link 16 and IFF Mode 5 upgrades will be delivered in RACR Release 1 (R1), with others following in successive releases to complete the fielding of these capabilities.

The Link 16 transmit capabilities included in F-22 Raptor Agile Capability Release (RACR) Release 1 will enable the two-way exchange of J-series messages (Link 16) between the F-22 and other Link 16-enabled aircraft, including the F-35A.

IFF modernisation was vital since aircraft without the latest available IFF standard have historically often been relegated to subordinate roles or have had to adhere to stricter rules of engagement, significantly reducing their usefulness and combat effectiveness. During the early years of the Vietnam war F-4 Phantoms frequently struggled to identify distant radar contacts and it was not until the introduction of the APX-80 IFF in 1972 that the F-4s were able to fully exploit their beyond visual range (BVR) capabilities.

The R1 increment of capability was due to start development testing in October 2019, but was delayed until the spring of 2020.

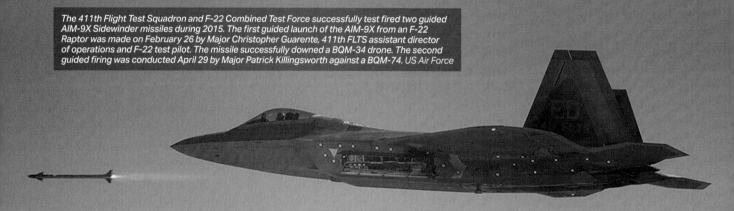

The 411th Flight Test Squadron and F-22 Combined Test Force successfully test fired two guided AIM-9X Sidewinder missiles during 2015. The first guided launch of the AIM-9X from an F-22 Raptor was made on February 26 by Major Christopher Guarente, 411th FLTS assistant director of operations and F-22 test pilot. The missile successfully downed a BQM-34 drone. The second guided firing was conducted April 29 by Major Patrick Killingsworth against a BQM-74. US Air Force

"In the event, there never was a Block 50, while both Block 40 and Increment 3 were rather more modest and Increment 3 was split into smaller packages which became Block 30 and Block 35."

> **"Lockheed Martin announced that it had completed 98 of 143 planned Block 3.2B upgrades by May 2021."**

*Lieutenant Colonel Wade Tolliver, the then 27th Fighter Squadron director of operations, released a 1,000lb GBU-32 Joint Direct Attack Munition over the Utah Test and Training Range on October 20, 2005, during a Combat Hammer air-to-ground weapons system evaluation programme exercise hosted by the 86th Fighter Weapons Squadron. US Air Force, Master Sergeant Michael Ammons*

The first flight of Raptor Agile Capability Release (RACR) Release 1 was achieved in February 2020.

Perhaps the most significant element of R1 is that it prepares the Raptor for the new AIM-260 JATM (Joint Air Tactical Missile) – the secretive new replacement for the AIM-120 AMRAAM. The F-22 is the threshold platform for the AIM-260 Joint Advanced Tactical Missile, whose existence was revealed in 2019, when it was forecast to be operational by 2022 or 2023.

Use of the JATM will reportedly be completely dependent on the RACR improvements, and the F-22 will need to have R1 embodied in order to use JATM at all, and to have the follow on R2 to fully exploit the new weapon's capabilities.

The open-system architecture provided by RACR may have the bonus benefit of facilitating the rapid integration of a commercial off-the-shelf helmet capability sooner than would have otherwise been possible. Integrating a fully interactive helmet that can cue the AIM-9X missile would still require extensive software changes, but using a one-way data stream, putting targeting information into the visor, is a potentially quicker solution that is being investigated. The Raptor test community is understood to be looking at three possible helmet solutions. The 422nd TES originally tested the Scorpion helmet mounted cueing system (HMCS) with the F-22 in 2014, but full integration was not funded amid reports that there were

difficulties with mapping the Raptor's cockpit, and inadequate clearance between helmet and canopy.

The second phase of RACR (RACR R2) has received approval and is now in operational testing. Primarily a software modification programme, Release 2 is understood to include a lot of JATM software, which will allow the pilot/vehicle interface to be refined and improved.

The air force and Lockheed are believed to be testing low-drag tanks and pylons as part of an effort aimed at increasing the Raptor's range, and there may be some associated

software within R2, though fielding of these new tanks is expected to follow RACR Release 2.

RACR Release 3 (RACR R3) is expected to follow about 12-18 months after the second RACR release, Lockheed's vice president for its Integrated Fighter Group, O.J. Sanchez, has said. Future F-22 modernisation will focus on datalink, sensor, and survivability enhancements in what is a rapidly evolving threat environment, and RACR R3 is expected to expand the Link 16 envelope, allowing message sharing between allied forces and will also see some upgrades to existing sensors.

*Alaskan-based Raptors became the first operational F-22s to drop GBU-39 small diameter bombs during a 2012 Combat Hammer exercise at Hill AFB. They provide a precision guided munition that can be carried in larger numbers than JDAM, and thus reduce collateral damage. US Air Force, Technical Sergeant Dana Rosso*

*An impression of an early LO external fuel tank design. The Raptor still lacks the ability to carry external fuel while remaining stealthy, though new LO tanks are being worked on. US Air Force*

## FUTURE UPGRADES

Ironically, in view of the fact that the type may have less than seven years to go before retirement, the F-22 looks set to enter one of the busiest periods ever when it comes to Raptor enhancements and upgrades.

Brigadier General Dale White, programme executive officer for fighters and advanced aircraft explained this apparent dichotomy, saying: "We still have a threat we have to address now. The F-22 represents our ability to address that threat, to be able to be the bridge to NGAD, and in order to do that, we have to keep it modernised. We have to keep it legal and operationally viable."

The US Air Force plans to spend $4.2bn in procurement in the fiscal year 2024-2028 period, with another $1.74bn 'to completion', circa 2030, as well as $3.2bn in research, development, test, and evaluation. This $9.06bn will see the F-22 through to the end of the decade, when, according to current plans, it is due to retire. These figures don't include operations and maintenance.

The overall quest is, according to the general: "how do we make the airplane do more, go farther, see farther?" It is perhaps no surprise that the biggest ticket items are 'sensor enhancement'

(with $4.13bn requested) and reliability and maintainability upgrades ($2.43bn requested).

Though the F-22's APG-77 radar has formidable LPI (Low Probability of Intercept) characteristics, it is still far from being an entirely passive and RF-free sensor, and this has increasingly been seen as being a significant missing element within the Raptor's sensor suite. An internal Infra-Red Search and Track (IRST) was planned for the F-22, but this - like the planned side-looking airborne radar (SLAR) arrays - fell victim to early funding constraints, and when the pre-production F-22 Raptor emerged it lacked an IRST. Since then, the internal space, power and cooling provision originally set aside for the equipment has been given over to other things, and installing an internal IRST would be an extremely complex and costly exercise, though an IRST is an increasingly attractive means of allowing the F-22 to operate outside the RF (radio-frequency spectrum) fight.

In 2017, Lockheed's then vice president for the F-22 programme, Ken Merchant, told *Air Force Magazine* that: "we really don't have the real estate," to fit an internal IRST in the jet, when asked why the aircraft could not be fitted with an equivalent to the Electro-Optical Targeting System (EOTS) used in the F-35.

The F-22 does have an AN/AAR-56 Missile Launch Detection system, or MLD, which provides the Raptor pilot with 360° detection of missile threats, using six optical sensors set behind low-observable windows. The AN/AAR-56's apertures are very small and could not form the basis of a useful EOTS type of sensor.

Other fighter types were able to use existing podded systems as IRSTs, including targeting

*This painting was posted on social media by General Mark D. Kelly, the head of Air Combat Command, and provides an interesting view of the highly classified AIM-260 Joint Advanced Tactical Missile, new stealthy fuel tanks and underwing IRST pods. The chisel-fronted pods have already been seen being flight-tested, but the tanks are new! US Air Force*

Maintaining low observable technology is critical to F-22 missions. Airman 1st Class Freddie Newman, a 325th MXS Low Observable apprentice, applies a layer of LO coating to an F-22 Raptor on July 1, 2013, at Tyndall Air Force Base. The 325th Maintenance Squadron helped to ensure that the F-22s at Tyndall maintained their stealth capabilities by maintaining and restoring the F-22's Low Observable coatings. US Air Force, Airman 1st Class Alex Echols

> "The philosophy underpinning RACR is for the F-22's software to be upgraded on an approximately annual cycle, sometimes with accompanying minor internal hardware changes achieved by using rapid prototyping."

pods like Litening III and Sniper that have been pressed into use for log range passive identification, and dedicated systems like the Legion pod. None of these could be used by the F-22 without compromising its Low Observability (Stealth).

Attention has therefore turned to the development of a podded Infra-Red Search and Track (IRST) system for the F-22. Budget documents suggest that an IRST Sensor Enhancement is due to come to the Raptor fleet with the full fleet due to be equipped by FY25.

The flagship of the 411th FLTS (06-0132) was photographed on approach to the Air Force's Plant 42 facility in Palmdale, California in early 2022 carrying a pair of faceted underwing pods with integral pylons. These pods had chisel-shaped fronts and were also shown in a rendering shared by General Mark Kelly on Instagram in April 2022. It is understood that one pod contains an IRST, and the other is simply ballasted to avoid carrying an asymmetric loadout.

Though the F-22 has four underwing hardpoints, these have seldom been used in frontline service. Each capable of carrying a 600 US gallon fuel tank or a pair of AIM-120 AMRAAM missiles, these hardpoints have never been cleared for use with air-to-ground weapons. This is because they compromise the F-22's radar cross section, to some degree even after being jettisoned, due to the resulting partially exposed connection points. This has meant that the tanks have largely been restricted to being used for ferry flights, or where low observability has not been required.

But with a growing emphasis on the Pacific theatre, and with the emergence of China's A2/AD strategy, range has become of ever greater importance. In order to ensure future mission execution, it was judged that it was now "critical to provide the Raptor with an increased range capability while maintaining own-ship survivability."

The US Air Force therefore intends to spend $553m on the F-22 Low Drag Tank and Pylon (LDTP) capability. Budget documents call for a total of 326 tanks and 286 pylons, which would give each aircraft at least two full sets of each.

These LDTPs are intended to provide greater range without affecting speed and manoeuvrability (unlike the existing external tanks) and in particular will provide a much-needed range boost in the Pacific theatre. They will still allow the F-22 to fly at speeds up to Mach 1.2 and will be equipped with smart rack pneumatic technology to accurately regulate ejection performance and ensure minimal drag and RCS even after jettison.

The LDTP's new efficient design would, it is said leave "very little, if any, radar cross-section disruption compared to a 'clean' F-22 once the tanks and pylons are jettisoned."

The new low-drag external fuel tanks and pylons could be integrated with other fighter platforms, such as the F-35, thereby significantly reducing the burden on the USAF's air-to-air refuelling tanker fleet.

These new tanks have not yet been seen 'in public' but were shown in the aforementioned picture shared on Instagram by General Mark Kelly. Rather than being of circular cross section the new tanks have a more 'flattened' and faceted appearance

Edwards-based Raptors have been involved in the AFRL SDPE's Autonomous Aircraft Experiment, flying with the VISTA F-16 (X-62), XQ-58 Valkyrie and MQ-28 Ghost Bat UAVs acting as surrogates for AI-controlled Collaborative Combat Aircraft (CCA). Video screenshot: US Air Force, AFRL SDPE

and are carried well forward on their supporting pylons.

One modification that does seem to be undergoing testing is a new 'mirrorlike' reflective metallic coating. Similar coatings appear to have been tested on the Scaled Composites Model 401 'Son Of Ares' demonstrators, on at least one F-117A and on a number of F-35s. The new coating was first noted on 04-4065, taking part in a Weapons School Integration (WSINT) sortie at Nellis Air Force Base on November 19, 2021, during the culmination of the USAF Weapons School's six-month Weapons Instructor Course. A second F-22 with a reflective coating (believed to be 04-4070) was spotted at Nellis AFB on March 17, 2022.

It is not known whether the new finish was applied to carry out some specific testing activity, or whether it is a new finish intended for the Raptor – or indeed for the forthcoming NGAD fighter. The finish may be intended as a replacement for the current rather delicate and maintenance intensive radar absorbent material now used on the F-22.

A test pilot commented that: "We are just trying to see if it's easier to maintain sustainability and reliability of the aircraft."

A host of areas have been identified for the F-22 Raptor upgrade and modernisation effort, including improved sensing (radar), combat identification, sensor fusion, new algorithms for 'optimised intercepts', synthetic data generation, a GPS-alternative navigation system, manned-unmanned teaming, pilot-assisted autonomy, cyber intrusion detection and prevention, predictive maintenance, Red Air threat replication, and real-time debriefing.

## STRUCTURAL AND MAINTENANCE UPGRADES

The F-22 has required unplanned modifications and upgrades for most of its service career – and before! The air force found structural cracks during fatigue testing that resulted in modifications to the aircraft's aft boom where the horizontal tail attaches to the fuselage. A second structural problem identified at an early stage was the discovery of cracking in titanium castings near the engine due to defects in the material delivered by a subcontractor.

A US Air Force F-22 Raptor and an F-35A Lightning II fly in formation with the Kratos XQ-58A Valkyrie low-cost unmanned aerial vehicle over the US Army Yuma test range during a series of tests in December 2020. The Valkyrie operated autonomously, taking its cues from the manned fighters with which it flew. US Air Force, Technical Sergeant James Cason

Quite separately, the air force planned a series of modifications to the structure in order to get to the planned 8,000-hour service life. These modifications were implemented under the Structural Retrofit Program (SRP), which cost $115m to modify 78 F-22As, and which took until 2010 to fully implement. The Structures Retrofit Plan (SRP) and a Reliability, Availability and Maintainability Maturation Program (RAMMP) that began in 2006 were finally completed in late 2020.

> "IFF modernisation was vital since aircraft without the latest available IFF standard have historically often been relegated to subordinate roles or have had to adhere to stricter rules of engagement."

Problems with the thermal management system impacted the F-22A's ability to operate in hot weather conditions, and the air force implemented a modification programme to correct these problems in early 2006.

A service life extension programme (SLEP) that would have increased the aircraft's design life from 8,000 flight hours to 10,000 or 12,000 hours was briefly considered, but analysis conducted under the F-22 Aircraft Structural Integrity Program (ASIP) determined that this would not be needed. Estimates indicated that each aircraft was flying around 360 hours annually and would therefore be capable of returning around 22 years of service. The greater use of simulators allowed flying hours to be reduced, thereby further extending the aircraft service life into the mid-2040s.

It now seems as though the F-22 will be retired before it has come close to 'using up' its service life.

Raptor 4007 of the 411th FLTS flies alongside the X-62, which is emulating a Collaborative Combat Aircraft during this sortie. The Autonomous Aircraft Experiment is a collaboration between the AFRL's Strategic Development Planning and Experimentation (SDPE) office, the 40th FLTS, the USAF Test Pilot School, and DARPA (the Defense Advanced Projects Agency). Video screenshot: US Air Force, AFRL SDPE

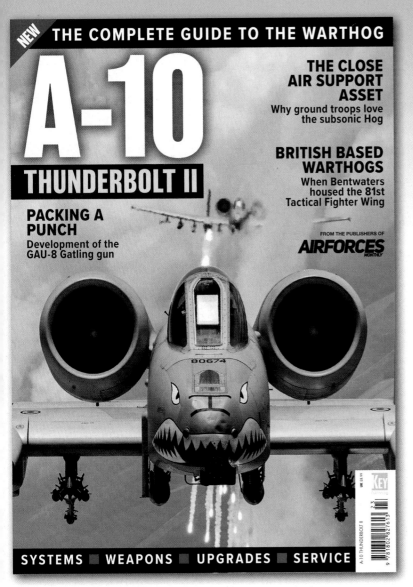

The first operational F/A-22 Raptor cruises over Florida on its delivery flight to Tyndall on September 29, 2003. Tyndall was the home of the world's first Raptor squadron, the 43rd Fighter Squadron, which functioned as the F-22 Formal Training Unit. *US Air Force, Technical Sergeant Mike Ammons*

# Pilot Training
## 2003-2018

**Although the Raptor force is small, the aircraft's formidable capabilities and reputation as the World's best fighter make what is something of an elite force a prized posting.**

AMERICAN HORNET
RAPTOR DRIVER

n the early days of the Raptor training programme, only experienced pilots who had distinguished themselves on other fighter aircraft types were eligible to be selected for F-22 training, and competition for a place was fierce.

Consequently, the first three F-22 squadrons to form (the 27th and 94th Fighter Squadrons at Langley AFB, and the 90th at Elmendorf AFB, Alaska) were somewhat 'top heavy' in terms of flying experience and qualifications, lacking what the British Royal Air Force calls 'First tourists'. Every pilot had flown another fighter platform before coming to the Raptor, and had been four-ship leads, and in some cases, had qualified as weapons instructors and/or flight commanders. To teach these 'old hands' to fly the F-22 was largely a matter of 'differences' training, and they were converted to the new

aircraft in a three-month transition course with the 43rd Fighter Squadron at Tyndall.

As the force continued to expand, it became clear that there would be a need to train some pilots fresh from undergraduate pilot training to fly the Raptor. There were some doubters at the beginning, with some scepticism as to the wisdom of taking students directly from pilot training and putting them in the F-22A with no prior fighter experience. But in the end, there did not seem to be any insurmountable obstacles, nor much alternative!

This naturally meant that Air Education and Training Command's 43rd Fighter Squadron at Tyndall had to revamp and redesign its course syllabus. The 43rd had been the first USAF squadron to operate the F-22A, and was

re-established at Tyndall AFB, Florida in 2002. The squadron's 15 Raptor Instructor Pilots began training 'student' Raptor pilots for the 27th Fighter Squadron at Langley AFB, Virginia in 2003, but all were experienced fighter pilots. One early 'customer' was the then air force chief of staff General John Jumper who, in 2004, became the first and only US Air Force service chief to qualify in the F/A-22. By 2007

*Major Michael Hoepfner completing his checkout flight in Raptor No.18 on January 14, 2004, becoming the first F/A-22 fighter pilot to finish his training at Tyndall. "I feel so lucky that I got to be the first to qualify," he said. Two previous Tyndall Raptor pilots, Lieutenant Colonel Jeffrey Harrigian, 43rd FS commander, and Major Steven Luczynski, a 43rd FS flight commander, both completed their training at Nellis Air Force Base, Nevada. US Air Force, Lisa Carroll*

it was time to embrace a new challenge – that of training 'greenhorn' Raptor drivers! "The good news of that is they don't have any bad habit patterns from other airplanes," Lt Col Derek 'Trapper' France of the 43rd Fighter Squadron observed. "The bad news of that is they don't have an experience base to draw on."

The syllabus for converting experienced F-15 and F-16 pilots to the F-22 was revamped. Lt Col David Krumm, 43rd Fighter Squadron commander explained that: "There are a lot more academics on how things work, why we do the things the way we do them, and a much more basic approach. There are more academics, more simulators and more flights."

The first thing was to test out the new seven month F-22 basic course, and after the instructors tested one another and assessed the syllabus, they sought input and advice from the instructors of Tyndall's 2nd and 95th Fighter Squadrons (which trained F-15 pilots) and from the A-10 FTU's instructors. The latter had long experience of converting ab initio pilots to a fast jet platform without having a two-seat trainer variant.

When other trainee fighter pilots take-off for the first time in their designated frontline aircraft type they will usually have an experienced instructor in the back seat, but when a young pilot gets airborne in an F-22 for the first time he is on his own. On his own, but not entirely inexperienced, having reached the 43rd FS after nearly two years of training on the T-6A Texan II and the T-38A Talon, plus a brief F-16 course. And he will usually be in a formation with his instructor. The instructor pilots of the 43rd FS may not be able to sit in the back seat of a two-seat training variant, because there isn't one, so instead they have become extremely skilled at monitoring their student from the position of being a flight lead, and at mastering the debrief!

> **"When a young pilot gets airborne in an F-22 for the first time he is on his own."**

But the first F-22 flight was still a big step. "You take a bunch of 22, 23, 24 year old lieutenants, and you hand them the keys to a $200 million dollar fighter, and the first time they're going to fly it they're solo… Was there any apprehension? That's the understatement of the year!" Lt Col Tom 'House' Kafka said.

### FOUR GO SOLO

It was intended that routine F-22 basic courses would begin in earnest by 2009, but before they did, the 43rd Fighter Squadron conducted a Small Group Tryout (SGTO), under which four pilots (1st Lt Austin Skelley, 1st Lt Ryan Shelhorse, 1st Lt Marcus McGinn, and 1st Lt Dan Dickinson) were put through the course. "We're really going to take a good hard look at what the course is and how they respond and how they perform during the time that they're here. We think we've probably got a 95% solution. But we know there's probably some things we need to tweak and correct," Col Krumm observed.

Following Undergraduate Pilot Training, the four pilots undertook the Introduction to Fighter Fundamentals Course on the T-38 at Randolph AFB, Texas. This was followed by a new, five-week Raptor lead-in course with the 63rd Fighter Squadron, part of the 56th Fighter Wing at Luke, flying two-seat F-16D Fighting Falcons (with an instructor in the back seat). This course was subsequently moved to Nellis Air Force Base in Nevada and then ceased altogether in about 2014. Eight F-16D flights allowed the pilots to experience flying a high-G, high performance aircraft with a fly by wire flight control system and a sidestick, and

*Major Max Maroska delivered 02-4028 to the 43rd Fighter Squadron on August 5, 2004, helping the training unit build up to full strength. The aircraft was the unit's seventh F/A-22A. US Air Force, Steve Wallace*

*Max Maroska is greeted and thanked by USAF Chief of Staff General John Jumper after delivering 02-4028 to Tyndall on August 5, 2004. Less than six months later, Jumper completed 50 hours of academics, five simulator sessions and three Raptor flights to qualify as a Raptor pilot himself. US Air Force, Lisa Norman*

*The first US Air Force F-22 Raptor Basic Course class graduated at Tyndall Air Force Base, on November 1, 2008. Colonel William H. Mott (centre), 325th Operations Group commander, stands with the four graduating student pilots, (left to right) 1st Lieutenant Daniel Dickinson, Captain Marcus McGinn, 1st Lieutenant Ryan Shelhorse and 1st Lieutenant Austin B. Skelly. US Air Force, Staff Sergeant Vesta M. Anderson*

included night flying, day and night landings, air-to-air refuelling and in going from the 6g T-38 to the 9g F-16 allowed them a useful opportunity to increase their ability to perform the anti-g straining manoeuvre!

These first four 'green' US Air Force pilots selected to fly the F-22 Raptor without

previous fighter experience joined the 63rd FS for the Raptor lead-in course on January 14, 2008, and arrived at Tyndall Air Force Base in February 2008, ready to begin a rigorous academics and simulator course.

The new students began flying the first of 160 F-22 conversion flights in March, and

the 43rd FS graduated its first four students from the new F-22 Basic Training Program on November 2, 2008. Since then, F-22 pilots have been chosen just like pilots for any of the USAF's other fighter platforms although the training does come with its own challenges.

The USAF's F-22 training system included pilot and maintenance trainers (simulators), instructor-led and student-paced courseware, and electronic classrooms. The pilot training system was developed by Boeing and employs three types of simulator: the Full Mission Trainer (FMT), the Weapons and Tactics Trainer (WTT) and the Egress Procedures Trainer (EPT). F-22 computer-based training uses state-of-the-art training technologies originally developed for the Boeing 777 commercial airliner.

The full-mission trainer features a high resolution, full 360o visual system, but is not motion based. It allows a pilot to practise the entire mission from engine start-up to engine shut down, and supports take-off and landing, formation flight training, air-to-air refuelling, emergency procedures, and within visual-range combat.

The PC-powered weapons and tactics trainers have a throttle and stick, and a limited visual system allows the pilot to practice individual and flight weapons employment and combat tactics only in a desktop environment. The WTT system can also be used for mission planning.

With these synthetic training devices, the 325th Training Support Squadron (TRSS) can actually provide more realistic combat training missions in the simulator than is possible by live flying in the actual airspace. This is, in part, due to the fact that in a secure synthetic

*Link has built and delivered F-22 pilot training devices, including full mission trainers, weapons tactics trainers and egress procedures trainers. Collectively, these pilot trainers are playing a key role in the F-22 training system. The F-22 Full Mission Trainer seen here consists of a fully populated cockpit on a fixed base and helps prepare pilots for solo flights in the Raptor by providing a high resolution, 360° virtual environment and supporting a complete range of tactical training scenarios. L3 Harris*

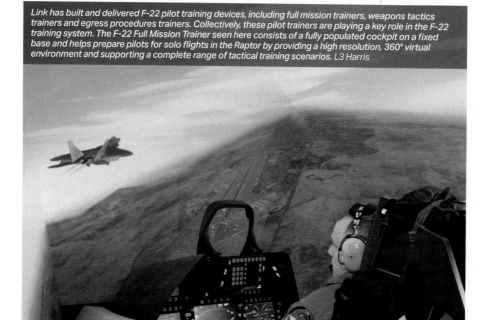

An F-22 Raptor from Tyndall Air Force Base touches down with a puff of smoke from its tyres on November 5, 2015. Students undergo an eight-month course of instruction with the 43rd FS, including 388 academic hours, 226 academics events, 26 examinations, 46 simulator missions and 37 flying sorties. US Air Force, Senior Airman Sergio A. Gamboa

environment, the Raptor's signature does not need to be artificially augmented, and its sensor performance does not need to be 'throttled back' in order to avoid compromising security to enemy satellites and SIGINT. Tyndall accommodated eight full mission simulators and 14 weapons and tactics trainer cockpits.

The F-22 basic course followed a five-block syllabus and could last for between seven and nine months. It included 380 hours of academic instruction and 45 simulated flight missions, as well as live flying. In the early days, a new F-22 pilot was expected to

complete 43 sorties, but the requirement was reduced to 38 in 2014.

Students had to pass all elements in order to successfully graduate the F-22 Raptor basic course, demonstrating proficiency in day and night time air-to-air refuelling and other syllabus areas. Three sorties are 'transition'; basic handling and navigation, which are followed by a practice check ride and then a formal check ride to pass the student fully qualified with the basic capabilities of the aircraft. These five flights account for 13% of the syllabus. Nine sorties (24%) were dedicated to BFM (Basic Fighter Manoeuvres),

and two to air-to-ground operations. The training aircraft do have JDAM (Joint Direct Attack Munition) capability but can only train for the SDB mission in the simulator.

Classroom studies, and simulator time were interspersed with live flying, culminating in a 'capstone' in which student pilots used the skills they had learned in a simulated combat environment.

The 43d FS's goal was to graduate 32 fully-qualified Raptor pilots each year, in four classes of approximately eight student pilots, with one instructor per student for all flight operations.

Lieutenant Colonel Tom 'House' Kafka, Florida Air National Guard Headquarters Det. 1 vice commander and 325th Training Support Squadron assistant director of operations, is the only pilot to have racked up 1,000 hours of F-22 flight time flying only from Tyndall. "I feel blessed, humbled, thankful and extremely lucky. I'm blessed because I still have the health to still be flying at the 25-year mark and lucky to be in the F-22 for going on ten years now," Kafka said. US Air Force, Senior Airman Alex Echols

# Training Post-Hurricane Michael

In 2018, Hurricane Michael wreaked havoc with the Florida coast. The devastation meant a rethink of F-22 operations.

A 325th Fighter Wing F-22A Raptor touches down at Eglin Air Force Base, on November 20, 2018, one of the first six Raptors arriving at their temporary home from Tyndall. This move was part of the US Air Force's Hurricane Michael recovery efforts at Tyndall. *US Air Force, Samuel King Jnr*

**B**y October 9, 2018, even as the approaching Hurricane Michael was given Category 5 status with peak winds hitting 160 mph, the USAF's fighter pilot training pipeline was already deep in a crisis of its own. The output of trained pilots from UPT was failing to keep pace with requirements, and the outflow of qualified pilots was not being adequately staunched by retention initiatives and bonuses.

By the end of fiscal year 2018, it was calculated that the US Air Force was short of 1,937 pilots. The situation was most acute among active duty fighter pilots – classed as those flying the A-10, F-15, F-15E, F-16, F-22A, and F-35 aircraft. Here, manning was at approximately 80% of total requirements, and the USAF was short of more than 1,000 fighter pilots.

A 325th Fighter Wing F-22A Raptor taxies off the runway at Eglin Air Force Base, in November 2018. The stay at Eglin was destined to be longer than many had anticipated! *US Air Force, Samuel King Jnr*

This crisis had been a long time in the making, and it was revealed that the US Air Force had fewer fighter pilots than were authorised in 11 of the 12 years between fiscal year 2006 and fiscal year 2017. The gap between pilots on strength and authorised strength grew from 192 fighter pilots (5% of authorisations) in fiscal year 2006 to 1,005 (27% of authorisations) in fiscal year 2017.

The crisis disproportionately affected the F-22 fighter community, because of its small size to start with. There were just 123 combat-coded aircraft in the primary mission aircraft inventory and fewer than 250 regular air force F-22 pilots plus an additional 40 full-time Air Reserve Component F-22 pilots actively serving. These numbers include all F-22 operational pilots, staff pilots, and instructor and student pilots.

By October 2018, only six of the 11 F-22 pilots eligible for the initial pilot bonus in FY18 had accepted it, indicating that five more F-22 pilots would soon leave the force, joining the 19 F-22 pilots lost during the year due to retirement, separation, or promotion to colonel.

It was recognised that all of this demanded the continued production of F-22 basic course students at the maximum rate. In recent years this had averaged 28 basic course pilots, 20 transition course pilots, and nine instructor pilots each fiscal year – and even this had proved not quite sufficient to prevent a slow but steady erosion in pilot numbers.

But if things were getting worse, they were at least getting worse slowly.

Off-duty maintenance crews were recalled to duty on the afternoon of Monday, October 8 to "spin up as many jets as they could to

A 43rd Fighter Squadron instructor pilot conducts a preflight inspection on an F-22 Raptor at Eglin Air Force Base, Florida, on February 1, 2022. The 43rd FS remained responsible for providing air dominance training for the F-22 Raptor until the FTU moved to Langley. *US Air Force, Airman 1st Class Tiffany Price*

fly, with the last ones launched on Tuesday morning." Thus 38 of Tyndall's 55 F-22s flew to other bases before the hurricane hit, most flying to Wright Patterson AFB in Ohio.

And then on Wednesday, October 10, Hurricane Michael hit the Florida Panhandle, devastating Tyndall AFB. Some 109 of Tyndall AFB's 484 buildings had to be demolished (26% of the total), all base housing was rendered unfit for occupancy, and some of the FTU's facilities were rendered unusable.

A stack of patches waiting to be presented to a graduating class of Raptor pilots. *US Air Force*

> "It was revealed that the US Air Force had fewer fighter pilots than were authorised in 11 of the 12 years between fiscal year 2006 and fiscal year 2017."

The remaining F-22s were those either undergoing planned maintenance or that could not be safely launched at such short-notice. These 17 Raptors (31% of Tyndall's F-22s) were designated non-mission capable (NMC) and were sheltered in place – which meant being left to ride out the storm.

These aircraft included four 43rd Fighter Squadron F-22s. One of these was scheduled to leave but GABed [ground aborted] after experiencing an issue before taxiing. Two had been cannibalised for parts and the other had issues that couldn't be quickly fixed.

Though there were some reports that some of the aircraft had been damaged beyond repair, this was not the case.

In fact, the 17 Raptors marooned at Tyndall survived the virtual destruction of the base and were brought back up to airworthy condition within days. Four aircraft needed replacement canopies and some aircraft needed replacement panels. Three aircraft required temporary repairs before they could be flown out. Most had damage to their LO coatings, but this did not prevent them from being flown. In some cases, spare parts were borrowed from the Joint Base Langley-Eustis fleet to allow the aircraft to be ferried to Joint Base Langley-Eustis for full repairs.

The 17 jets aircraft had all been relocated to different bases by November 16, 2018, and all had been repaired and returned to full flying status by April 2019. That was the good news.

Robin Olds' book, *Fighter Pilot* was also presented to graduating F-22A pilots. *US Air Force*

## REASSIGNMENTS

There was no good news for the 95th Fighter Squadron, whose personnel and Raptors were reassigned to other F-22 units at JB Langley-Eustis, JB Elmendorf-Richardson, and JB Pearl Harbor-Hickam before the squadron was unceremoniously disbanded. In December 2018, Air Force Secretary Heather Wilson said: "We have recommended that the best path forward to increase readiness and use money wisely is to consolidate the operational F-22s formerly at Tyndall in Alaska, Hawaii and Virginia."

The 43rd Fighter Squadron survived, at least initially, though the impact of the hurricane halted F-22 pilot training in its tracks for two months, further exacerbating the pilot shortage that the air force was already facing. The F-22s of the 43rd Fighter Squadron and the T-38 aircraft of the associated 2nd Fighter Training Squadron temporarily relocated to Joint Base Langley-Eustis in Virginia, though it actually relocated to Eglin AFB, while definitive plans were drawn up. This relocation disrupted the student pilot full-rate basic course that had been taking place at the time.

When Hurricane Michael struck Tyndall AFB, the F-22 FTU was training 14 basic course students, with two track two students, and a single track one attendee enrolled in training.

The track one student (a current fighter pilot who had not previously flown the F-22) had completed the majority of his training and went to his operational unit to complete his transition. The two track two students (previously qualified F-22 pilots who were no longer current) had not started their training, and returned to their gaining operational units which assumed the resource burden and risk for training them.

The 14 students on the basic course were approximately 90 days into their 160 day journey, but had, on average, completed only eight of the 38 flying sorties in the syllabus, and had no option than to somehow complete the course. It seems that some thought may have been given to relocating the FTU to Langley straight away, but with a need to restore training of replacement pilots via the F-22 FTU by January 31, 2019, this was not a viable option. Joint Base Langley-Eustis had no F-22 FTU instructors and lacked the simulators that were available at Tyndall AFB, a full 895 miles away, by road.

It quickly became clear that there were no real alternatives to restarting academic and synthetic training at Tyndall and standing up the flying element of the FTU at nearby Eglin AFB.

This was because two very important facilities for the F-22 FTU had survived the destruction wrought by Hurricane Michael

at Tyndall AFB: the Special Access Program (SAP) flight simulators and the low observable maintenance facility.

The Academic Simulator Building (ASB) at Tyndall AFB served as the hub for all F-22 FTU instruction, supporting more than 68% of the F-22 basic course syllabus including academic lessons, computer based instruction, and using the eight full mission simulators and 14 weapons and tactics trainer cockpits. The ASB received minimal damage from the hurricane and was quickly restored to full operational capability.

It was calculated that moving the SAP simulators from Tyndall AFB to any other location would take at least a year and cost $22m, which would have further disrupted the training pipeline just when such delays were least manageable.

Meanwhile Eglin AFB's main airfield (Eglin Main) was only about 90 miles away from Tyndall AFB and had sufficient ramp space and operating capacity to accommodate the F-22 FTU's flying operations. It was also close to the Special Use Airspace previously used by the 43rd Fighter Squadron in the Gulf of Mexico.

The FTU relied on a substantial workforce of instructors and maintenance personnel, many of whom were contractors, civilian employees, and Air Force Reserve and Guard personnel who were unable or unwilling to relocate, not

A US Air Force F-22 Raptor (02-4033) assigned to the 43rd Fighter Squadron takes off from Eglin Air Force Base, Florida, on February 1, 2022. *US Air Force, Airman 1st Class Tiffany Price*

*"The 17 Raptors marooned at Tyndall survived the virtual destruction of the base and were brought back up to airworthy condition within days."*

F-22A Raptors (01-4024 and PRTV II aircraft 00-4012) from the 43rd Fighter Squadron fly alongside a KC-135 Stratotanker during a refuelling mission over the Florida Panhandle, on December 14, 2022. The 43rd Fighter Squadron operates the F-22 basic course which trains student pilots on the fighter fundamentals, including air-to-air refuelling. US Air Force, Technical Sergeant Betty R. Chevalier

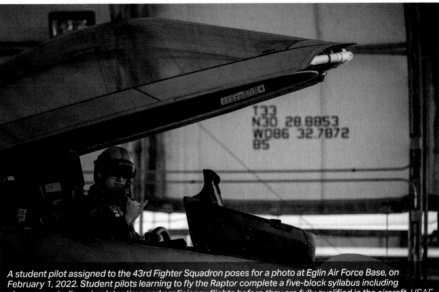

A student pilot assigned to the 43rd Fighter Squadron poses for a photo at Eglin Air Force Base, on February 1, 2022. Student pilots learning to fly the Raptor complete a five-block syllabus including classroom studies, simulator time and proficiency flights before they are fully qualified in the aircraft. USAF

least because they needed to attend to the repair of their own homes. Air Force Reserve and Guard personnel made up 25% of the F-22 FTU's instructor pilots.

All of this made a split FTU operating from Tyndall and flying from Eglin the only near-term alternative that would allow the F-22 pilot production pipeline to be quickly re-established. The F-22 FTU restarted limited student flying at on December 6, 2018, after a gap of nearly two months.

With 90 miles separating the FTU's flightline from its simulators, the syllabus had to be modified. Previously, students would spend a day or two in the simulator and then move to fly the exercise in the aircraft before going back to the simulators or classroom.

Major 'Icarus', the 43rd FS assistant director of operations, said: "We've had to completely rethink how we do the F-22 B-course. Ultimately, we've tested both approaches. Having the students go back and forth from one installation to the other with the old syllabus and remaining in one place for an entire block with the new syllabus. The students do just as good with both."

## SPLIT COURSES

Under the new syllabus the students complete all classroom and simulation blocks at Tyndall and then moved to Eglin for the remainder of the course. This provided more stability to both the staff and students, obviating the need

A 43rd Fighter Squadron F-22 Raptor (02-4030) taxies at Eglin Air Force Base, Florida, on March 22, 2023. The F-22 B-course, which has been hosted by the 325th Fighter Wing since 2002, is now moving to Joint Base Langley-Eustis, where the FTU will be the 71st Fighter Squadron. US Air Force, Senior Airman Tiffany Del Oso

to bounce back and forth, and significantly boosting morale.

But even as the new syllabus was introduced in January 2019, it was always clear that the split Tyndall/Eglin FTU was only an interim solution, and that the air force wanted to consolidate Raptor training at Langley, further concentrating its overall F-22 fleet. While the Special Use Airspace previously used by the 43rd Fighter Squadron in the Gulf of Mexico was becoming busier, Virginia's bipartisan, bicameral congressional delegation pointed out in 2019 that: "The East Coast mid-Atlantic training ranges provide an excellent opportunity to train with other fourth- and fifth-generation aircraft in the region."

A formal proposal to move the FTU to Langley was made in March 2019, subject, of course, to the inevitable environmental impact study.

The air force finally notified Congress that the study was complete in June 2021, and proposed that the FTU's 28 F-22s and 16 T-38s would move to Langley, along with approximately 760 personnel, 660 of them USAF personnel.

The 1st Fighter Wing at JBLE redesignated the 71st Fighter Training Squadron, up to then equipped with T-38. The unit became the 71st Fighter Squadron in November 2022, in preparation for its new mission as the F-22 FTU. The 71st Fighter Generation

Squadron was activated on January 6, 2023, and on January 20, General Mark Kelly, the commander of Air Combat Command, signed a memorandum directing the stand-up of the F-22 Raptor Formal Training Unit at Joint Base Langley-Eustis, Virginia.

A ground-breaking ceremony was held for a new low-observable composite repair site in 2022, while work on a new combined maintenance and operations facility began on February 22, 2023.

The phased transfer of the new unit's F-22s (which came from the 325th Fighter Wing at Eglin AFB) began in March 2023, and all 30 aircraft were expected to be in place by September 2023.

The first two F-22 Raptors for the 71st Fighter Squadron (tails AF040 and AF042, already wearing Langley's FF tail code), arrived at Joint Base Langley-Eustis, Virginia, on

Wednesday, March 29, 2023, piloted by Lt Col Andrew 'Lite' Gray, commander of the 71st Fighter Squadron and Lt Col Matthew Evers, the unit's director of operations.

"We're going to train pilots who just got their wings, how to employ the F-22 in our squadron, and then we'll send them out to their combat units," said Lt Col Gray.

The first cohort of six students for the 71st Fighter Squadron spent three months undertaking classroom lessons and simulator sorties at Tyndall AFB before arriving at Langley, where they flew their first F-22 training flights on June 5, 2023.

The FTU course will continue to be divided between Tyndall and Langley for some time, with three months of classroom and simulator training at Tyndall followed by six months of flying at Langley, and this will continue until new facilities are built at

Colonel Christian Bergtholdt, the 325th Operations Group commander, and Colonel Brad Huebinger, the 1st Operations Group commander at Joint Base Langley-Eustis, make their way to their aircraft at Eglin Air Force Base on July 25, 2023. Tyndall's current fleet of aircraft are being reassigned to the 1st Fighter Wing. US Air Force, Staff Sergeant Stefan Alvarez

"If the Block 20s are retired, then at least one current frontline squadron will have to give up its aircraft for training – and perhaps even two."

*Lieutenant Colonel Matthew Evers, 71st FS director of operations, taxies one of the first two 71st Fighter Squadron F-22s to arrive at Joint Base Langley-Eustis, Virginia, on March 29, 2023. Evers and Lieutenant Colonel Andrew Gray, 71st Fighter Squadron commander, flew the first two aircraft (02-4040 and 02-4042) from Tyndall Air Force Base, Florida to Langley where they were assigned to the 71st, the new home of the F-22 Formal Training Unit. US Air Force, Senior Master Sergeant Amy Robinson*

Langley, which will take at least three years to get up and running.

In the meantime, the 325th Fighter Wing at Tyndall and the 1st Fighter Wing will share the task of training budding F-22 pilots to provide air superiority anywhere around the globe. Captain Spencer Bell, a 71st Fighter Squadron flight commander said that the training phases delivered at Langley were: "Designed to get the pilots from not knowing anything about the airframe to graduating and being our next air dominance professionals.

"The whole intent behind the course is to not only be able to fly the F-22 but be able to effectively employ it. We send people off to Combat Air Force squadrons, who are ready to deploy and ready to do the mission."

The future of the actual F-22 airframes the students are flying remains uncertain. The US Air Force has said that it wants to retire all 32 of its Block 20 F-22s now used for training,

*A student pilot assigned to the 71st Fighter Squadron conducts his first F-22 flight (in 02-4033) during the basic flying course at Joint Base Langley-Eustis, Virginia, on June 5, 2023. The nine-month long course is designed to take the students from not being able to fly the F-22 to being the USAF's next generation of air dominance professionals. US Air Force, Technical Sergeant Ceaira Tinsley*

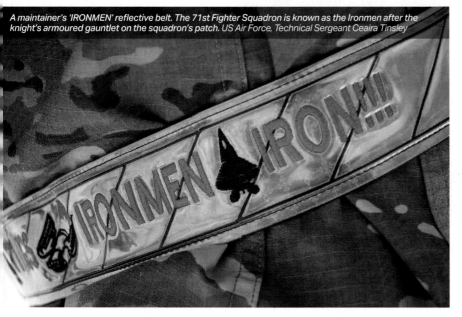

*A maintainer's 'IRONMEN' reflective belt. The 71st Fighter Squadron is known as the Ironmen after the knight's armoured gauntlet on the squadron's patch. US Air Force, Technical Sergeant Ceaira Tinsley*

because they are too costly to maintain, not representative of the combat-coded fleet, and cannot be rated for combat themselves.

In testimony before the House Armed Services Committee's tactical aviation panel, on March 29, Lt Gen Richard G. Moore Jr., vice chief of staff for plans and programs said the Block 20 aircraft were so out of synch with the combat-coded Block 35s that pilots were receiving "negative" training from them, meaning that they were having to "unlearn" habits developed in the Block 20 before they could become proficient in the Block 35.

But Congress has so far specifically prohibited the service from retiring any F-22s until at least 2027 under last year's National Defense Authorization Act, and there has so far been no sign that lawmakers might repeal that proviso this year, allowing divestment of the Block 20s.

If the Block 20s are retired, then at least one current frontline squadron will have to give up its aircraft for training – and perhaps even two. This could mean the end of Raptor operations in Hawaii, or even in Alaska.

# Raptor Diversity

The US Air Force prides itself on being open to all and race, gender or service should present no obstacle to earning a place in the cockpit of an F-22 Raptor.

n the 21st century US Air Force it should come as no surprise that there have been high calibre African American Raptor drivers – including at least one high profile Raptor Demonstration Team pilot, Major Paul 'Loco' Lopez. Another black F-22 pilot was Major Daniel 'Fuzz' Walker, who appeared on *Real Talk*, a military issues webcast that streamed on Facebook, hosted by Lieutenant General Brad Webb. The session was a platform to discuss race, diversity, and inclusion in the air force, and Walker (the grandson of a wartime Tuskegee Mustang pilot, Norman Scales) said that he had hoped that as an F-22 pilot, his race

Paul 'Loco' Lopez is the highest profile African American Raptor pilot – having led the Raptor Demonstration Team. A former F-15 pilot, Lopez attended the F-22 Raptor transition course at Tyndall AFB in January 2011. He flew F-22 Raptors with the 27th Fighter Squadron at Langley AFB until October 2012, when he moved to Joint Base Elmendorf-Richardson flying Raptors there until January 2016. Moving back to Langley AFB in January 2016 Lopez served as the chief of flight safety for the 1st Fighter Wing and was selected as the Raptor demonstration pilot, a role he fulfilled until 2019. *US Air Force*

Former F-15E pilot Dawn Dunlop was assigned to Edwards AFB as the F-22 Operations Officer from 2003–2005. She later became the vice commander and then commander of the 412th Test Wing. Her subsequent career attracted controversy, with accusations that she had created a toxic environment when serving as director of the Special Access Programs Control Office. *US Air Force*

would not change the way he was treated. But during F-22 training, the ebullient Walker was admonished for being too loud. On his first squadron, having changed his 'loud' personality to 'fit in' he was told he was too quiet!

After 11 years in the air force, Walker tired of what he called this "uphill battle" and left the USAF for Harvard Law School. This left the US Air Force with fewer than 50 black pilots. General Webb, now the commander of the Air Education and Training Command described his departure as: "A loss for the air force. He was an incredible pilot, an incredible officer, an outstanding officer for us."

There have also been a handful of female F-22 pilots (four according to some sources, but at least six), including Major General Dawn Dunlop, Major (now Lt Col) Jammie 'Trix' Jamieson, Major Nichole 'Vapor' Ayers, Captain Nichole 'Fire' Bahlman, Captain Elizabeth 'Craps' Pennell, and a major known only by her Christian name and callsign, Chelsea 'Contra'.

This is perhaps unsurprising, as there are many more female fighter pilots across the US Air Force 11F career field (103) than there are African Americans as of 2022.

Originally trained as an F-15E pilot, Dunlop was later assigned to Edwards AFB as the F-22 operations officer from 2003–2005, converting to the Raptor. She later became the vice commander and then commander of the 412th Test Wing, before retiring as director, operational capability requirements in the Deputy Chief of Staff for Strategic, Integration, and Requirements in November 2021.

The first operational female fighter pilot selected to fly the Lockheed Martin F-22 Raptor was Captain Jammie Jamieson, an F-15C pilot who completed the F-22A Transition Qualification Course in 2008, and who went on to fly the Raptor operationally with the 525th Fighter Squadron. Jamieson is now a colonel, serving with the 412th Operations Group.

Major Nichole 'Vapor' Ayers began flying the T-38A in the adversary squadron at Langley Air Force Base, Virginia, providing combat training for the F-22 Raptors at Langley. She then graduated from the F-22 basic course in 2018 and became an instructor pilot in the F-22. She has flown over 200 combat hours in Operation Inherent Resolve over Iraq and Syria, of more than 1,150 total flying hours in the T-38A/B/C and F-22 Raptor and led the first-ever all-woman F-22 formation in combat in 2019. At the time of her selection as a NASA astronaut candidate in late 2021, she was the assistant director of operations in the 90th Fighter Squadron at Elmendorf Air Force Base, Alaska.

While Dunlop, Jamieson and Ayers are no longer flying the F-22 on the frontline, other young women are.

*The commander of the Air Education and Training Command described 'Fuzz' Walker as: "an incredible pilot, an incredible officer, an outstanding officer." Walker began his USAF career full of enthusiasm and pride but ended it tired of this "uphill battle" leaving the cockpit of the F-22 for Harvard Law School. US Air Force*

*Jammie 'Twix' Jamieson (Right) was the first operational female F-22 Raptor pilot, and in March 2023 met Captain Elizabeth 'Ellie' Pennell – the latest member of this exclusive club. By 2022 there were 103 female fighter pilots across the US Air Force 11F career field. US Air Force*

> ## "At the time of her selection as a NASA astronaut candidate in late 2021, she was the assistant director of operations in the 90th Fighter Squadron at Elmendorf Air Force Base, Alaska."

*Jammie Jamieson, callsign 'Trix', was the first operational female fighter pilot selected to fly the Lockheed Martin F-22 Raptor, completing the F-22A Transition Qualification Course at Tyndall in 2008. She came to the F-22 after three years flying the F-15C. US Air Force*

Captain Elizabeth Pennell is an F-22 Raptor pilot assigned to the 90th Fighter Squadron, and who recently paid generous tribute to Jamieson, saying: ""I'd like to say thank you, for what you have done as a senior officer and how the obstacles you overcame have made it easier for me in my career field as a fellow aviator. I haven't really faced any barriers and it's because of women like you that made that possible."

Another current female Raptor pilot is Major Chelsea of the 94th Fighter Squadron, stationed at Joint Base Langley-Eustis as an instructor pilot, going by the callsign 'Contra'. 'Contra' is probably the most experienced woman Raptor pilot today, having qualified in 2014.

A recent USAF video seemed to suggest that another serving Raptor pilot may be Lieutenant Elena Dent, while the Air National Guard can boast Captain Nichole 'Fire' Bahlman. The grand-daughter of a former naval aviator who flew the TBF Avenger and SBD Dauntless during the Battle of Midway, the Douglas A-1 Skyraider, and the F-86 Sabre in Korea, Bahlman originally rode horses competitively while in high school and college and pursued a career in finance to support herself as a professional equestrian competitor. But when one of her top horses was injured, she switched to her current job, becoming the first female fighter pilot in the Hawaii National Guard.

*Left and below: Major Nichole 'Vapor' Ayers became an instructor pilot in the F-22 as well as flying more than 200 combat hours in Operation Inherent Resolve over Iraq and Syria. She also led the first-ever all-woman F-22 formation in combat in 2019. She went on to become a NASA astronaut candidate in late 2021. US Air Force*

Lieutenant Colonel Kevin Horton, a former commander of her squadron remembered that: "'Fire' represented herself as extremely resilient, with an unbelievable amount of self-belief and ability to adapt and conquer, which is absolutely crucial in our line of work."

Bahlsen herself says: "The F-22 Raptor is a compelling platform that requires expertise and careful handling to be used to its full potential. Similarly, women have had to navigate a complex environment to succeed, requiring determination, skill, and resilience.

"Just as the Raptor is still being studied and improved every day to adapt to a changing environment, women continue to learn and grow in their roles, adapting to new challenges and progressing towards a more equitable and inclusive society. It is up to us to continue to support and empower women, just as we must continue to study and develop the Raptor to ensure its full potential."

But perhaps the most surprising minorities (albeit not from minorities that have suffered much discrimination) represented on the Raptor force are white men – from the UK and Australia! Given the tight security surrounding what is still a highly classified aircraft, it is perhaps surprising that there are long-running exchange pilots with the British Royal Air Force, and with the Royal Australian Air Force, under which British and Australian pilots get to fly the F-22 for three years, while USAF exchange officers trade places with them to fly the Eurofighter Typhoon and F/A-18E Super Hornet.

Joking aside, it was a natural progression to integrate coalition partners into a Raptor exchange process. For the coalition, the benefit of the exchange programme is that both US and British warfighters and planners will better understand the Raptor's and Typhoon's potential and capabilities, with significant advantages on both sides.

The UK RAF F-22 exchange began at an early stage of the programme, with the first

Captain Nichole 'Fire' Bahlman is an F-22 pilot with the Hawaii National Guard, one of a number of young women currently flying the Raptor but probably the first in the National Guard. Bahlman is seen here giving the *shaka* or 'hang loose' hand gesture - often associated with Hawaii and surf culture but widely adopted by fighter pilots. *US Air Force*

British pilot to complete F-22 Raptor training graduating on July 17, 2006. The 29 year old Flight Lieutenant Dan Robinson was a Tornado F.Mk 3 pilot with No.25 Squadron, who had applied for the US Navy F/A-18 Super Hornet exchange programme. Instead, Robinson was told he was going to the F-22 Raptor. "I didn't even know that the Raptor exchange programme existed or that I was up for it. I couldn't believe it," he said.

Major Mike Cabral, 43rd Fighter Squadron chief of weapons and tactics said that apart from dealing with a few "phraseology challenges", Robinson had been an outstanding student and would be a true asset to the Raptor programme once flying with his squadron at Langley. "Once we got him his decoder ring for US speak, he was good to go. Fighter pilots are fighter pilots," Maj Cabral said. "With his combat skill set, it was a seamless transition. He has coalition operations and weapons instructor experience; he will be a force multiplier." During his exchange, Robinson had the distinction of landing the first Raptor in the UK, leading a three-ship of F-22s which took part in the Royal International Air Tattoo (RIAT) and the Farnborough International Airshow in 2008. After leaving the RAF, Robinson moved to the USA and founded Red 6 Aerospace, a Santa Monica-based defence tech company that has developed the Airborne Tactical Augmented Reality System, (A-TARS).

Since Robinson, there has always been a Brit on the Raptor force. In 2021, there were briefly two, as Squadron Leader Alex 'Thorney' Thorne prepared to return to the UK and Squadron Leader David Wild prepared to take over.

Towards the end of his tour in 2021, Squadron Leader Thorne had been one of the pilots who participated in a flypast as part of the unveiling of the National World War One Memorial in Washington DC on April 20, 2021.

Drago formation's communications were recorded, and on approaching the memorial, Thorne was heard to say: "Drago two to Drago one. As a British officer serving with the US Air Force, it's a great honour to fly over this wonderful memorial with you and recognise the huge sacrifice made by the United States in World War One - thank you."

With a second RAF officer serving on the 94th Fighter Squadron, the two pilots seized the opportunity to make the first formation flight by F-22 Raptors ever flown by Royal Air Force pilots, on June 15, 2021.

Lieutenant Commander Mike 'WooG' Wosje, had more than 2,100 flying hours in the F/A-18 when he started flying test and evaluation missions in the Raptor with the 59th Test and Evaluation Squadron at Nellis in 2006. *US Air Force*

Ben 'Duzza' Durham was the RAF F-22 exchange officer from 2015-2018, initially assigned as a flight commander on the 94th Fighter Squadron. In early 2017 he was appointed director of operations and second-in-command of the squadron. Durham subsequently orchestrated and led the squadron's Operation Inherent Resolve deployment, flying missions over Syria and Iraq. For his contribution to this deployment, Durham was appointed MBE and won the Royal Air Force Museum American Foundation (RAFMAF) Sword of Honour for 2018. *US Air Force*

"What do I think of my time with the 94th? Best adventure of my life!"

Two years after the first British pilot joined the Raptor force, Australia began its own Raptor exchange, when Squadron Leader Matthew Harper began his three-year assignment to the 90th Fighter Squadron at Elmendorf in the spring of 2008, becoming the flight commander in charge of scheduling and training.

Alex 'Thorney' Thorne in the cockpit of 'his' 94th FS Raptor. Thorne was the fifth RAF Raptor pilot, following Dan Robinson (2006-2009), Jon Smith (2009-2012), Guy Lockwood (2012-2015), and Ben Durham (2015-2018). *US Air Force*

The formation used the callsign 'Fiske' in honour of William Meade Lindley 'Billy' Fiske III, a US volunteer who fought for (and gave his life in) the Royal Air Force during the Battle of Britain.

"I'm here, flying your apex fighter, in a programme that's highly classified, in a jet that's highly classified, ready to deploy with you and serve your great nation at any moment," Thorney said. "I don't think many other people do that. I don't think many countries have that

level of trust…More important than me, more important than this unit, I think it's a symbol of how closely we work together."

Of his historic formation flight, Thorne observed: "It was surreal. The first time I ever flew an F-22 I couldn't believe the power and significance of what that moment meant.

"But to fly in a Raptor, instructing an old buddy from home, that I hadn't flown with since I was his instructor on the Typhoon weapons instructor course, was awesome!

Alex 'Thorney' Thorne and David Wild pose with a Union Flag after their historic 'Brit Raptor formation' flight. Wild took over the exchange in 2021. *US Air Force*

"Australia has a history of having an exchange pilot with the 90th back when they flew F-15Es," Harper explained. "When the (squadron) transitioned to the F-22, the position was continued, allowing the first Australian to fly the F-22."

Harper has been followed by a succession of fellow RAAF pilots, the latest being Flight Lieutenant Bryce 'Wooly' Woollett, who joined the programme in mid-2020.

The final 'minority' on the Raptor force allegedly has webbed feet – and consists

RAAF Hornet pilot Squadron Leader Matthew Harper began his three-year assignment to the 90th Fighter Squadron at Elmendorf in the spring of 2008. US Air Force

"The UK RAF F-22 exchange began at an early stage of the programme, with the first British pilot to complete F-22 Raptor training graduating on July 17, 2006."

From top to bottom: Harper was followed as the Aussie Raptor exchange pilot by Flight Lieutenants Mark Biele (2011-14), William 'Gradz' Grady (2014-2017), Paul 'Ando' Anderton (2017-2020), and Bryce 'Wooly' Wollett (2020-23). US Air Force

of the US Navy (and USMC) pilots who have flown the F-22!

An exchange between the USAF's 422nd Test and Evaluation Squadron and the Naval Strike and Air Warfare Center at Naval Air Station Fallon, Nevada began in 2006, with a TOPGUN instructor brought in to fly the F-22. The first such officer, Lieutenant Commander Mike 'WooG' Wosje, had more than 2,100 flying hours in the F/A-18 when he started flying test and evaluation missions in the Raptor with the 59th Test and Evaluation Squadron at Nellis.

One of his first tasks was to fly one of the newest Raptors to come off the line at Marietta, Georgia. "It was like that new-car smell once you step into the cockpit, and without a scratch on it," he said.

Lieutenant Colonel Daniel Holmes, commander of the 59th TES, said of Wosje that: "When the chief of staff of the air force and chief of naval operations made the decision to bring a navy pilot into F-22 operational test, they picked the right guy. We not only gained joint service support for the F-22 programme, but also enhanced all future testing and combat operations in the air force, navy and marines."

Wosje said that one of the challenges he had faced was one of: "Speaking air force. I grew up operating and talking in a maritime-air environment and that has hindered the process of communicating to air force members. But hopefully, before I leave, I'll have a full understanding so I can bring all the knowledge I learned back to the navy side."

Holmes jokingly confirmed this communications problem, saying: "I have

found myself looking around to see if I'm the only one who didn't understand what he said! But before the navy comes and steals 'WooG' back for themselves to keep, we have him for another three years, enabling us to pick his brain and enhance our joint operations and stealth tactics for years to come!"

The initial 'port/starboard' plan had called for the US Navy and Marine Corps to alternate sending a pilot to Nellis. Thus, Wosje was followed by a US Marine, David Berke, who explained that the timing was carefully managed. "The timing made perfect sense because the Marine Corps was anticipating standing up its F-35B fleet in the early 2010s, and the leadership wanted to get someone with fifth-generation experience so we could hit the ground running as opposed to starting cold. The marines thought the best way to do this was to work this alternating plan with the navy."

But after Berke completed his tour and the navy's Eric Doyle assumed the role, the US Marines ended its participation in the scheme, having worked out their own exchange with the USAF to send a pilot to the F-35A community.

Berke, therefore became the only marine to have ever operationally flown the F-22. For a brief period of time, when he commanded VMFAT-501 at Eglin AFB he was also the only pilot in the world who had operationally flown both the F-22 and F-35.

The exchange became a navy-only affair, and Doyle was followed by Erick 'Pol Pot' Kammeyer, Blaine 'Convict' Felony, and Chris 'Penguin' Case, all of whom were former TOPGUN instructors.

# SUBSCRIBE

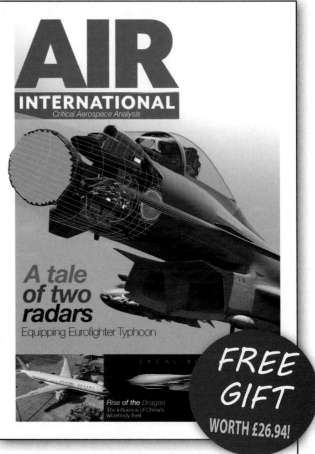

# TODAY

*Airforces Monthly* is devoted entirely to modern military aircraft and their air arms.

**shop.keypublishing.com/afmsubs**

*Combat Aircraft Journal* is renowned for being America's best-selling military aviation magazine.

**shop.keypublishing.com/casubs**

ing.com

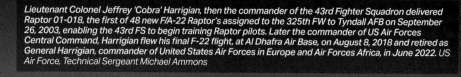

Lieutenant Colonel Jeffrey 'Cobra' Harrigian, then the commander of the 43rd Fighter Squadron delivered Raptor 01-018, the first of 48 new F/A-22 Raptor's assigned to the 325th FW to Tyndall AFB on September 26, 2003, enabling the 43rd FS to begin training Raptor pilots. Later the commander of US Air Forces Central Command, Harrigian flew his final F-22 flight, at Al Dhafra Air Base, on August 8, 2018 and retired as General Harrigian, commander of United States Air Forces in Europe and Air Forces Africa, in June 2022. US Air Force, Technical Sergeant Michael Ammons

# Fleet Organisation

From a lofty original ambition of fielding 750 F-22s, regular USAF budget reductions saw a total force of fewer than 200. Jon Lake looks at where and why they are based.

The US Air Force originally envisaged a production run of 750 F-22s, which would have allowed replacement of the F-15C on a virtually one-for-one basis. This number was reduced to 648 in 1991, though it was then still intended that the air force would station 40% of the operational fleet outside the United States. The US DoD's 1993 Bottom-Up Review further reduced the planned number of production F-22s to 438 (plus four pre-production versions, later reduced to two).

The total of 440 F-22s was judged to be sufficient to equip four F-22 fighter wings in a total USAF force structure of 20 wings which would comprise 13 active wings and seven Reserve/National Guard organisations.

The 1997 Quadrennial Defense Review (QDR) again reduced the planned number of production F-22s to 339 aircraft, which was sufficient to support three F-22 fighter wings in a slightly changed 20-wing force structure (12 active; 8 Reserve/National Guard).

The requirement was reframed further as the US Air Force reorganised its air power into ten air and space expeditionary force (AEF) packages, each of which would require a 24-aircraft F-22 squadron. With test and training aircraft and a modest attrition reserve, this led to an official USAF requirement for a PMA (Primary Mission Authorised) figure of 240 – which equated to 381 aircraft.

Meanwhile, the air force sought to work out where to bed down the initial three-squadron F-22 operational wing. The USAF wanted to use an existing Air Combat Command (ACC) base, with Langley AFB, Virginia as its preferred option, but with four alternative locations under consideration. These were Eglin AFB, Florida; Elmendorf AFB, Alaska; Mountain Home AFB, Idaho; and Tyndall AFB, Florida. At Eglin, Elmendorf, additional since the F-22s were to replace operational F-15Cs,

while at Tyndall AFB, a new, separate wing would be formed that would be additional, since there were no operational F-15C aircraft to drawdown. Nellis AFB was also considered.

Further reductions eventually brought the total down to 187 production aircraft. This figure was arrived at when, in late 2004, Presidential Budget Directive 753 removed production funding for the F-22 after FY 2008, effectively ending production at 183 F-22s. Just four extra aircraft were authorised above this total.

The first US Air Force F/A-22 Raptor (PRTV II aircraft 00-4012) was delivered to the 422nd Test and Evaluation Squadron at Nellis Air Force Base, Nevada on January 14, 2003. Raptor 12 - the 12th F/A-22 built - was initially used to teach operational test pilots and maintenance personnel how to fly and repair the aircraft safely and effectively. AWFC pilots then used the aircraft and seven more F/A-22s assigned to the unit, to develop the tactics, techniques, and procedures for the entire combat air forces. US Air Force, Staff Sergeant Colette M. Horton

## LOW NUMBERS

This meant a PMA availability of aircraft of only about 120 – half of that originally required, and insufficient to support all ten air and space expeditionary force packages, or indeed all of the bases that had been considered as locations for the first F-22 wing.

Eglin AFB was selected as the location for F-35 Joint Strike Fighter pilot training of all US Air Force, Navy, and Marine personnel as part of the 2005 Base Realignment and Closure Act (BRAC) which meant that it did not meet the requirements for hosting an F-22 operational wing. Similarly, and as a result of the same act, Mountain Home AFB became the primary location for F-15E aircraft assets. These additional missions meant that Mountain Home also did not meet the requirements for hosting an F-22A operational wing.

Nellis AFB continued to have unique FDE requirements for one squadron of F-22As and two proposed squadrons of F-35s to support testing, training, and weapons system evaluation, which also ruled it out as a location for an operational F-22 wing. And it was decided that training would be centred at Tyndall, leaving Elmendorf as the obvious host for the second operational wing.

The reduction in F-22 orders from a high of 750 aircraft to fewer than 200 forced an

*F/A-22 flight testing with the 411th FLTS began in 1997 with Raptor 4001, the first EMD F-22, and eight more EMD jets assigned to the 411th FLTS would participate in the test programme. Here, four of the squadron's F/A-22 Raptors fly over the Mojave Desert during a landmark test mission. A record number of seven Raptors were airborne simultaneously during several test missions on August 29, 2003. US Air force, Kevin Robertson*

> "It was decided that training would be centred at Tyndall, leaving Elmendorf as the obvious host for the second operational wing."

immediate reassessment of plans for their deployment, with much smaller wings. It was initially decided that there would be four such wings, at Langley in Virginia, Holloman in New Mexico, Tyndall in Florida, and Elmendorf in Alaska, with small numbers of aircraft in Hawaii and test/development aircraft at Nellis in Nevada and Edwards in California.

In 2006, the air force decided to organise its F-22s into seven operational squadrons, each with 18 primary mission aircraft. The primary

wings at Langley, Elmendorf, and Holloman would each have two frontline squadrons (plus an associate unit with no aircraft of its own), while Tyndall was to have the FTU and a single squadron. With the test community and the inexplicable outpost in Hawaii, this meant that squadrons would be limited to fewer than 20 aircraft each – many of which would inevitably be undergoing maintenance or repair at any one time. Even under the most optimistic plans, *F-22 squadrons* were authorised to

*Brigadier General Larry New, commander of the 325th Fighter Wing at Tyndall Air Force Base, leads a formation of four F-15C Eagle fighters from the 1st, 2nd, and 95th Fighter Squadrons and the 325th Operations Group, together with a single F/A-22 Raptor from the 43rd FS. US Air Force, Master Sergeant Michael Ammons*

Above and left: Major Charles 'Corky' Corcoran, a 27th Fighter Squadron Fighter Pilot, takes off in a F/A-22 from Langley Air Force Base, Virginia on January 28, 2005. This was the first F/A-22 sortie from Langley flown by a Langley-based pilot, though the newly delivered aircraft still wore Tyndall's TY tail codes. US Air Force, Staff Sergeant V. Levi Collins

have only 18 to 21 Primary Aircraft Assigned (PAA) compared to 24 PAA for legacy fighter squadrons.

The F-22 force was clearly going to be very thinly spread, and it was not long before there was a major rethink.

By 2010, the air force was acknowledging that its basing plan was unsustainable because its operational squadrons were not able to conduct adequate sorties. So, on June 29, 2010, the Department of the Air Force announced plans to consolidate the F-22 fleet, acknowledging a need for fewer bases, each with larger numbers of aircraft. There did not seem to have been any serious consideration given to cancelling the stand-up of the units in Hawaii, though the relatively small number of aircraft would seem to have been better deployed to one of the bigger CONUS-based wings.

The air force decided to eliminate one squadron and to use some of the aircraft from that squadron to increase the number of primary mission aircraft to 21 in its five

remaining active duty squadrons. They also left the single F-22 National Guard squadron with 18 primary mission aircraft.

At the time, Kathleen Ferguson, deputy assistant secretary for installations explained that: "This plan maximises combat aircraft and squadrons available for contingencies. By consolidating aircraft at existing bases, F-22 operational flexibility is enhanced."

Officially, consolidation saw the F-22 force go from six squadrons with 18-21 aircraft each to five squadrons with 24 aircraft.

Teams surveyed four F-22 bases, evaluating them according to the feasibility, timing, cost, and planning required for them to accept additional F-22 aircraft. It was said that the secretary of the air force and the chief of staff of the air force carefully considered the site survey results (including appropriate environmental analysis) and military judgment factors before making their basing determinations.

It was determined that the most effective basing for the F-22 required redistributing aircraft from one F-22 squadron at Holloman to units at the remaining four F-22 bases, and to relocate the second squadron at Holloman to Tyndall AFB.

At Holloman, the 8th Fighter Squadron was deactivated, and its aircraft were dispersed with six going to Langley, six to Elmendorf, and two to Nellis. The remaining squadron – the 7th Fighter Squadron - was relocated to Tyndall, re-numbering as the 95th Fighter Squadron.

Thus, by 2015, the force consisted of 157 Primary Aircraft Authorised (PAA) – 48 at Langley (two 24-aircraft squadrons), 36 at Elmendorf (two 18-aircraft squadrons),

"The Hawaii ANG have stated that increasing their squadron complement by just four additional aircraft would enable the squadron to generate 32% more sorties."

Lieutenant Colonel James Hecker, the 27th Fighter Squadron commander, delivered the first operational F/A-22 Raptor to its permanent home at Langley Air Force Base, Virginia, on May 12, 2005, escorted by a pair of F-15Ds – one of them carrying photographer Ben Bloker! US Air Force, Technical Sergeant Ben Bloker

20 with the single squadron at Hickam, and 53 at Tyndall – 24 each with the 43rd and 95th Fighter Squadrons, and five with the 301st. Langley, Elmendorf and Hickam's associate units had no aircraft assigned.

By May 2018, the two Langley squadrons each had 23 aircraft, while Elmendorf's had 24 (90th FS) and 23 (525th FS). There were still 20 aircraft in Hawaii, while Tyndall had 55 (31 with the 43rd FS and 24 with the 95th FS). Finally, four aircraft were allotted to the 412th Test Wing at Edwards, and 14 to the 53rd Wing at Nellis.

But the F-22 fleet was considerably smaller than these figures might suggest, suffering poor availability rates that consistently lagged behind the USAF's required 'availability standard'. It had been alleged that the force would struggle to support combatant commander needs.

## AIRCRAFT AVAILABILITY STANDARD

The USAF Aircraft Availability standard is based on the air force's evaluation of requirements, including operational and training requirements, and is not resource constrained. In 2012-2016, for example, the Aircraft Availability standard for the F-22 was 66.7% for fiscal year 2012, was set at 72.6% in fiscal year 2015, and was 72% in fiscal years 2016 and 2017. During that period, the actual F-22 fleet availability rate was four to 19% lower than the air force's annual F-22 availability standard. In Fiscal Year 2016 the average number of F-22s available for operations was just 80, from a total inventory of 186 aircraft. F-22 availability has generally lagged behind that of the USAF's fourth generation fighters by 10-20%, thanks in part to the increasing maintenance demands of the aircraft's ageing Low Observable coatings.

In FY 2021, availability rates for the USAF's 4th generation fighters ranged from 66.24% for the F-15E to 71.53% for the F-16C, while the F-35A showed 68.8% (according to Lockheed Martin data in the latter case) and the A-10 72.54%. The F-22 had an availability rate of just 50.81%.

It is widely recognised that the USAF's fourth generation fighters are themselves currently underperforming in terms of availability due to an intense modification schedule, heavy maintenance requirements, and a lack of aircraft due to deployments.

The small size of the F-22 fleet, combined with low availability, has significantly reduced the type's combat effectiveness. This has been further exacerbated by poor organisation and management of the fleet, which, according to the US Government Accountability Office (GAO), has not maximised the availability of these 186 aircraft. This is a particular problem, as only five of the air force's 55 combat coded fighter squadrons are equipped with the F-22, and yet the type is acknowledged to be the only USAF fighter capable of achieving air superiority against the most advanced air and surface threats in the most contested environments.

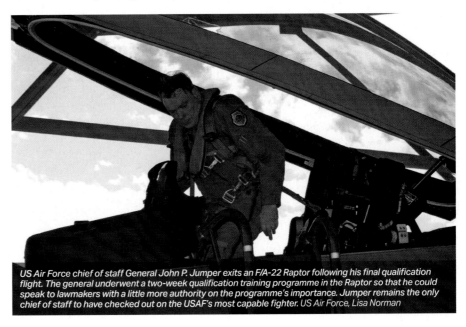

US Air Force chief of staff General John P. Jumper exits an F/A-22 Raptor following his final qualification flight. The general underwent a two-week qualification training programme in the Raptor so that he could speak to lawmakers with a little more authority on the programme's importance. Jumper remains the only chief of staff to have checked out on the USAF's most capable fighter. US Air Force, Lisa Norman

A 411th Flight Test Squadron F-22 Raptor from Edwards AFB, California undertook a three-week deployment to Eielson Air Force Base, Alaska for cold-weather testing of its braking system, testing the Raptor's ability to manoeuvre, stop and go on slippery surfaces. The aircraft was tested on incrementally low-level runway condition reading surfaces, with temperatures ranging between 37o to minus 13o. US Air Force, Kevin Roberston

> ## "F-22 pilots need extensive training in order to be prepared to execute their highly specialised and vital mission, and they are not getting enough of that training."

Many would like to see steps being taken to improve F-22 availability, and to focus the force's activity where it is most needed. According to the GAO, this is not the case today.

In a 2018 report to congressional committees, the GAO charged that: "F-22 organisation and utilisation changes could improve aircraft availability and pilot training."

The GAO said that the air force's organisation of its small F-22 fleet had not maximised the availability of these 186 aircraft, which was constrained by both maintenance challenges and unit organisation. Maintenance of the F-22's low observable coatings has always been challenging, soaking up more resources than was ever expected. The F-22's LO coating is actually a series of coatings that require diligent and time-consuming application and curing, resulting in extended periods of time in maintenance. The F-22's

LO coating has an eight to 10 year life span, but this can be reduced by as much as three years by environmental factors including high temperatures, humidity, and salinity. The air force has taken action to address this by using a more durable coating and by standing up additional LO repair facilities, but still does not house its F-22s in climate-controlled hangars at three of the four operational locations (Alaskan F-22s do use such hangars), and they are thus exposed to these LO degrading environmental factors. As the F-22's LO

coating nears the end of its service life, it requires complete replacement.

F-22 availability has also been constrained by supply chain issues. The F-22 fleet's small size means that there is a relatively low demand for parts, and relatively low inventory levels. Obtaining missing parts can be time-consuming and costly due to DMS (diminishing manufacturing sources) problems, with some original equipment manufacturers no longer making parts and others being out of business altogether. When this is the case, the air force has to locate the original design plans, and then find and commission a new contractor to produce what may be a small number of parts, sometimes requiring a lengthy redesign and requalification process. Because of this, even a simple wiring harness can require a 30-week lead time. There is also a shortfall of spare engines.

### SMALL UNITS
These maintenance challenges have been exacerbated by the USAF's decision to organise the F-22 fleet into small units, often with just 18-21 primary mission aircraft per squadron and with one or two squadrons per wing. Traditional USAF fighter wings have three squadrons per wing with 24 aircraft in each squadron, which creates maintenance efficiencies because people, equipment, and parts can be shared.

F-22 aircraft availability has fluctuated but has generally been better for operational locations with more aircraft per squadron and with more squadrons per wing. Thus, both

Representatives from the US Air Force and Lockheed Martin gathered to see the roll-out of Pacific Air Forces' first F-22 Raptor on February 12, 2007, at Marietta, Georgia. This F-22 was the first assigned to PACAF at Elmendorf Air Force Base, Alaska, with 'AK' tail codes and a Pacific Air Forces badge on the tailfin. US Air Force, Angela Tyson

Carrying underwing fuel tanks, the 302nd Fighter Squadron's 'flagship' intercepts a Russian Tupolev Tu-95MS Bear-H strategic bomber during a routine mission from Elmendorf on November 22, 2007. *US Air Force*

Langley and Elmendorf have enjoyed higher aircraft availability rates than the locations with only one operational squadron – Hickam and Tyndall – and were also generally able to generate more sorties per month.

Perhaps surprisingly, the frontline squadron at Tyndall seems to have been unable to leverage the maintenance benefits of also having the F-22 training squadron 'on base'. This is in part because the F-22s at the training squadron were among the oldest F-22s in

the fleet and were maintained at a different configuration than the operational aircraft. Historically, F-22s used for training had not been required to have fully maintained LO coatings but a change in that requirement resulted in a large maintenance backlog for these training aircraft as their coatings had to be restored, dramatically impacting availability at Tyndall.

Although there are many factors that influence F-22 maintenance and availability

statistics including aircraft age and use, climate and unit leadership, there is no doubt that larger squadrons and wings have a significant effect on availability.

It has been calculated that relatively small increases in aircraft can leverage significant improvements in availability. The Hawaii ANG have stated that increasing their squadron complement by just four additional aircraft would enable the squadron to generate 32% more sorties.

Here two F-15 Eagles (an F-15E off the Raptor's starboard wing and an F-15C to port) fly alongside an F-22A Raptor and an A-10 Thunderbolt II over Tucson, Arizona, on Sunday, March 5, 2006. *US Air Force, Airman 1st Class Veronica Pierce*

Colonel Jeff Harrigian, by now the 49th Fighter Wing commander, and Lieutenant Colonel Mike Hernandez, commander of the 7th Fighter Squadron, fly a pair of F-22A Raptors over White Sands National Monument, on their way to Holloman Air Force Base, New Mexico, on June 2, 2008. These aircraft were the first two Holloman-tailed F-22s to arrive on base, though Holloman's time as an F-22 base was destined to be brief. US Air Force, Senior Airman Russell Scalf

squadrons to a single forward location – usually a major air base. In the face of a growing threat and faced by China's A2AD (Anti-Access/Area Denial) capabilities, this started to look inflexible and limiting. If fighters can deploy only from one well-known base to another well-known base, then they will be predictable and vulnerable, no matter how technically advanced and operationally capable they might be in the air, and no matter how tactically skilled their crews might be.

Instead of operating from well-developed and vulnerable major air bases, it is now planned that squadrons or UTCs would break up into smaller units and operate independently from multiple locations, moving around in order to complicate enemy targeting

To facilitate exactly these kind of operations, Air Force Pacific Command developed the Rapid Raptor concept which has since been expanded from a theatre-specific capability to a global one by Air Combat Command and is now being spread across the tactical aviation fleet as the Agile Combat Employment model.

Under the so-called Rapid Raptor concept, a package of four F-22 Raptors and supporting logistics, fuel, and munitions, with at least one C-17 Globemaster III aircraft, would quickly deploy to any forward operating base in the world (including non-traditional locations and austere bases), and would be refuelled, rearmed and combat-ready within 24 hours of deployment, all with a smaller footprint.

But while Rapid Raptor promises unprecedented flexibility in the deployment of fifth-generation fighter aircraft, there are real doubts as to whether the F-22 force has

Ironically though, the air force has made a deliberate practice of deploying relatively small elements of its Raptor squadrons as Unit Type Codes (UTCs). An F-22 UTC will typically take six of a squadron's 21 aircraft but will take 60% of its operational personnel, 50% of the squadron's equipment, and approximately 40% of the squadron's maintenance personnel, making it more difficult for the undeployed portion of the squadron to maintain readiness and generate sorties. Moreover, while these UTCs may have a disproportionate share of personnel and equipment they will often also be allocated a squadron's best aircraft, its more experienced personnel, and critical parts.

Traditional fighter squadrons typically have larger UTCs, with a better balance in equipment and personnel between deployed and undeployed elements.

Larger UTCs are better able to meet emerging DoD concepts for using distributed operations in high threat environments. In the past, the air force tended to deploy its

> "Though homeland defence is naturally a top priority for the DoD, it does not require the F-22, and other types would be better suited to it."

An F-22A takes off at Holloman Air Force Base, on October 22, 2008, for training missions in the local area. This was the first time that Holloman had launched a pair of F-22s. US Air Force, Technical Sergeant Chris Flahive

An F-22 Raptor from Joint Base Pearl Harbor-Hickam, Hawaii, lands at Andersen Air Force Base, Guam, during exercise Resilient Typhoon, April 22, 2019. The exercise is designed to validate Pacific Air Forces ability to maintain readiness while adapting to rapidly evolving events. The 'Hawaiian Raptors' consist of airmen from the Hawaii Air National Guard's 154th Wing and their active-duty counterparts from the 15th Wing. US Air National Guard, Senior Airman John Linzmeier

> *"Shortages of dedicated adversary aircraft often meant that F-22 pilots had to fly their aircraft as simulated adversaries to support the training of their squadron mates."*

sufficient availability and maintainability to execute the strategy.

Perhaps even more importantly, there are real concerns as to whether Raptor pilots are ready to undertake these kinds of operations. The GAO found that the air force's utilisation of its F-22 fleet has limited its pilots' opportunities to train for their high-end air superiority missions, and that it has contributed to F-22 pilots not meeting their training requirements.

The high-end air superiority role – seizing and maintaining air superiority (and ideally air dominance) in a high threat environment is extremely demanding, and as fourth generation fighters become progressively less survivable, more of the burden will fall on the small fleet of F-22s.

The Raptor's role can be divided into three. The primary missions consist of Offensive Counter-Air (OCA) and Defensive Counter-Air (DCA). The OCA mission (once known as Escort/Sweep) entails defeating enemy fighters and escorting other fighters or bombers over hostile territory. Conversely, DCA is focused on defending friendly airspace against air threats, including enemy fighters, bombers, and cruise missiles. The F-22 also has the secondary mission of Air Interdiction/Offensive Counter-Air/Attack Operations, an air-to-ground mission to defeat and eliminate advanced surface-to-air missile threats and other ground targets that contribute to an enemy's air power.

But F-22 pilots need extensive training in order to be prepared to execute their highly specialised and vital mission, and they are not getting enough of that training.

## ADVERSARY AIR

A US Air Force analysis undertaken in 2016 concluded that, based on current aircraft availability rates, pilots in an F-22 squadron with 21 primary mission aircraft on strength would need 270 days of home station training each year to meet their minimum annual continuation training requirements, but found that they were actually only getting 191 days on average. This meant that they were not fully prepared to effectively support combatant commander needs against the most advanced threats. And these requirements are the minimum - some pilots may need additional sorties to achieve proficiency.

Why then, are squadrons failing to deliver this home station training?

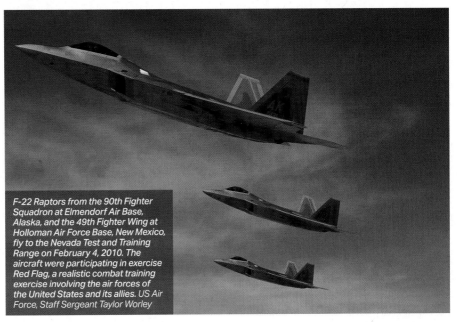

F-22 Raptors from the 90th Fighter Squadron at Elmendorf Air Base, Alaska, and the 49th Fighter Wing at Holloman Air Force Base, New Mexico, fly to the Nevada Test and Training Range on February 4, 2010. The aircraft were participating in exercise Red Flag, a realistic combat training exercise involving the air forces of the United States and its allies. US Air Force, Staff Sergeant Taylor Worley

## F-22 SQUADRONS

7th FS, 49th Wing, 2008-2014
8th FS, 49th Wing, 2009-2011
19th FS, 15th Wing, ANG, 2010-date
27th FS, 1st Fighter Wing, 2003-date
43rd FS (FTU), 325th Fighter
    Wing, 2002-2022
59th TES, 53rd TEG, 2004-date
71st FS (FTU), 1st Fighter Wing,
    1/2023-date
90th FS, 3rd Fighter Wing, 8/2007-date
94th FS, 1st Fighter Wing, 6/2006-date
95th FS, 325th Fighter Wing, 2013-2019
149th FS, AFRC, 1st Fighter Wing, ANG,
    10/2007-date
199th FS, 15th Wing, 2010-date
301st FS, 325th Fighter Wing,
    AFRC, 2010-2023
302nd FS, 3rd Fighter Wing, AFRC,
    10/2007-date
411th FLTS, 412th Test Wing, 1998-date
422nd TES, 53rd TEG, 2004-date
433rd WS, 57th Wing, 2004-date
525th FS, 3rd Fighter Wing, 10/2007-date
6511th TS, 6510th Test Wing,
    1989-91 (YF-22)

*Above and below: Lieutenant Colonel Shawn Anger, commander of the 7th Fighter Squadron, led the first five F-22 Raptors that left Holloman for Tyndall Air Force Base on January 6, 2014. Colonel Anger had flown the F-22 since 2004, and was the 33rd military pilot to fly the aircraft. He later became the 354th Fighter Wing commander and flew his final flight on retiring on August 15, 2020. US Air Force, Airman 1st Class Aaron Montoya*

Tyler Rogoway, on his excellent *The Warzone* website concluded that: "The USAF is wasting F-22s on patrols and deployments," and that: "the jets and their pilots are too busy with missions that don't require their unique capabilities to prepare for conflicts that do."

The GAO found that F-22 units were too often directed to participate in relationship-building exercises with partners, which provided little training value to the F-22 pilots, who are often restricted from flying the aircraft the way they would in combat, due to security concerns and an unwillingness to expose the F-22's unique capabilities. F-22 pilots could even develop 'bad habits' that then had to be corrected in future training.

Even when Raptor pilots are undertaking the required 'home station training' there are concerns that it may not be as effective or as useful as it should be. The US Air Force expects F-22 pilots to face and defeat numerically superior adversaries, and continuation training requires those pilots to fly against multiple aircraft playing the role of adversaries.

The USAF has assessed that there is an annual demand for between 145 and 171 adversary air sorties for every operational F-22 pilot – a much higher number than is required by fourth generation fighter pilots.

Those flying the USAF's other air superiority fighter are assessed as requiring just 45-73 adversary air sorties. To help meet the demand, the USAF has dedicated T-38 adversary squadrons at Langley and Tyndall, while Elmendorf's F-22s use the services of an F-16-equipped adversary squadron at a nearby base. Insufficient adversary air caused pilots to have shortfalls in their training at all F-22 operational locations, and at Tyndall in 2016 it was reported that this had negatively impacted the training of 83% of the squadron's pilots for the offensive counter-air mission and 54% of the pilots for the defensive counter-air mission.

Moreover, shortages of dedicated adversary aircraft often meant that F-22 pilots had to fly their aircraft as simulated adversaries to support the training of their squadron mates. Such sorties are assessed as being useful only for maintaining basic flying proficiency, and as having no value - or even negative training value for the pilots flying as adversaries! In 2017, it was estimated that 55% of the sorties generated by F-22s based in Hawaii were dedicated to adversary air.

Even more of a problem is the diversion of F-22s to support current combatant commander needs, even where these needs contribute nothing to F-22 training requirements and could be better met by other tactical aircraft platforms. Sometimes, F-22 deployments seem to be motivated more by a desire to 'spread the load' and to ensure that difficult and unpopular deployments are 'shared around', rather than on the basis of sensible and considered matching of resources to tasks.

Thus, the F-22 force has been deployed to a number of combatant commands to address a variety of needs, including providing assurance to friends and allies and deterring potential adversaries, but always having the consequence of reducing the time available for F-22 pilots to conduct home station training for their high-end air superiority missions.

Since 2007, the Air Force has deployed F-22s to the US Central Command area of responsibility (AOR) to support ongoing operations against the so-called Islamic State (ISIS) in Iraq and Syria. This has provided pilots with experience of deploying for combat,

Hurricane Michael led to further change for the F-22 force, with Tyndall's frontline unit standing down, and the FTU operating from Eglin. Here an F-22 Raptor assigned to the 325th Fighter Wing undergoes pre-flight checks at Eglin Air Force Base, Florida, on January 28, 2021. Student pilots were conducting night flying training to familiarise themselves with low-light operations. US Air Force, Staff Sergeant Stefan Alvarez

of integrating with coalition forces, and of conducting air-to-ground attack operations, but at the cost of letting F-22 pilot air superiority skills degrade while on deployment. Moreover, the air-to-ground attack operations carried out have tended to be close air support (CAS), which is not a primary or secondary mission for the F-22. But battling ISIS does not require the F-22's unique capabilities, nor does it help to prepare F-22 pilots for their primary (or secondary) missions.

Another responsibility that takes time away from vital air superiority training is the air sovereignty alert mission. Though homeland defence is naturally a top priority for the DoD, it does not require the F-22, and other types would be better suited to it, while it does further reduce opportunities and time for F-22 pilots to train for the high-end air superiority mission. In other parts of the United States, F-15C and F-16 squadrons routinely fill alert mission requirements, and many believe they should replace the F-22 alert commitment, too.

The air sovereignty alert mission requires a participating air base to maintain a number of fully fuelled, fully armed aircraft (with their pilots)

sitting alert in order to fulfil a 24-hour per day alert commitment. Squadrons must dedicate a number of mission-capable aircraft to this mission, and while on alert, neither pilots nor aircraft can train for their primary and secondary missions. F-22s are maintained on alert full time at Hickam and Elmendorf, while Langley is assigned alert missions on an as-needed basis.

The alert mission does not require the high-end capabilities provided by the F-22 and though these missions are important, they could easily be performed by other fighter types.

A further consolidation of the F-22 fleet is currently underway in 2023, as the wing formerly based at Tyndall winds down, redistributing aircraft from the disbanded 95th Fighter Squadron, and from the AFRC 301st Fighter Squadron to Langley and Elmendorf, and moving the FTU (formerly the 43rd Fighter Squadron) to Langley (where it was renumbered as the 71st Fighter Squadron).

If the USAF does succeed in divesting 32 early-model F-22s, it is hard to see the existing force structure surviving unscathed, and there may be further squadron disbandments.

The first two F-22 Raptors for the new F-22 FTU touch down at Joint Base Langley-Eustis, Virginia, March 29, 2023. The Formal Training Unit is transitioning from Tyndall to Langley, which will see the bed down of 30 additional F-22 Raptors and the establishment of a new FTU. US Air Force, Airman 1st Class Mikaela Smith

# 1st Fighter Wing

## Langley Air Force Base, Virginia

**THE 1ST FIGHTER WING** (1 FW) is stationed at Langley Air Force Base, VA (now known as Joint Base Langley-Eustis) and is assigned to the Air Combat Command's Fifteenth Air Force.

The Wing's 1st Operations Group (1st OG) is a successor organisation to the 1st Fighter Group, one of the 15 original combat air groups formed by the US Army before World War Two. The 1st OG is the oldest major air combat unit in the United States Air Force, originally formed on May 5, 1918.

The 1st Fighter Wing is responsible for one third of the USAF's combat-coded F-22 Raptors and is tasked with delivering F-22 air power worldwide on short notice to support Combatant Commander taskings.

In 2005, the Wing's 27th and 94th Fighter Squadrons became the first squadrons in the world to achieve operational status flying the

F-22 Raptor. The first Raptor assigned to the Wing had arrived on January 7, 2005, but was allocated as a maintenance trainer. The second Raptor, designated for flying operations, arrived on January 18, 2005. On December 15, 2005, the 27th Fighter Squadron was declared as fully operational and capable to "fly, fight and win with the F-22." The unit was the first operational F-22 Raptor Wing to take part in a major theatre exercise, Northern Edge 2006.

In addition to operating and maintaining these two F-22 Air Dominance squadrons, the wing is standing up a new FTU, the 71st Fighter Squadron, and also flies the T-38 as adversary air to increase training capability.

The 1st Fighter Wing boasts that it "leads the way in combat capability and lethality in current operations worldwide, and serves as America's premier Air Dominance wing, led by next generation airmen, integrated with its

*A crew chief talks to 1st Fighter Wing F-22 Raptor pilots after they landed at Hickam Air Force Base, Hawaii on February 7, 2007. The wing flagship is in the background. The F-22s were bound for Kadena Air Base, Japan, for the aircraft's first overseas operational deployment. US Air Force, Technical Sergeant Shane A. Cuomo*

mission partners, and ready to fly, fight, and win...anytime, anyplace."

The maintainers of the 1st Fighter Wing claim to: "set the standard for low observable and aircraft maintenance, both of which establish the unit as the most capable and combat ready F-22 wing in the air force."

Under a major USAF realignment, Langley AFB and Fort Eustis were consolidated into Joint Base Langley-Eustis, which stood up in January 2010.

On February 4, 2023, F-22s of the 1st Fighter Wing were dispatched from Langley AFB to shadow an alleged Chinese spy balloon that had been floating southeast over the continental United States for several days. Once the balloon floated over the Atlantic Ocean near South Carolina, one of the F-22s fired a single AIM-9X Sidewinder air-to-air missile at the balloon from an altitude of 58,000ft, downing it. The wreckage landed approximately six miles offshore and was subsequently secured by ships of the US Navy and US Coast Guard. The downing of the balloon marked the first air-to-air kill made by an F-22.

*An F-22 Raptor (08-4162) assigned to the 1st Fighter Wing, Joint Base Langley-Eustis, takes off for a sortie at Royal Air Force Lakenheath, England on October 9, 2018. Instead of a tail code and serial, some so-called 'flagship' Raptors have their unit designation on the fin, with the serial displaced to the fin fillet. The Raptors were training with US allies and partners as part of a demonstration of US commitment to European regional security. US Air Force, Senior Airman Malcolm Mayfield*

*Helmets belonging to pilots from the 71st, 94th and 27th Fighter Squadrons, prior to the 2023 William Tell fighter competition. US Air Force, Technical Sergeant Matthew Coleman-Foster*

# 27th Fighter Squadron

## 'Fightin' Eagles'

**THE 27TH FIGHTER SQUADRON** is equipped with the F-22 Raptor and forms part of the 1st Operations Group located at Joint Base Langley–Eustis, Virginia. The 27th Fighter Squadron is the oldest active fighter squadron in the United States Air Force, having amassed more than 100 years of service to the nation. It was originally organised as the 21st (later 27th) Aero Squadron on May 8, 1917 at Kelly Field, Texas. The squadron deployed to France during World War One and fought as a pursuit squadron on the Western Front. One of its pilots was Frank Luke, Jr., the 'Arizona Balloon Buster', who was credited with 18 kills and who became the first airman to be awarded the Congressional Medal of Honor.

After a long and distinguished career in World War Two and beyond, in 2003, it was announced that the 27th Fighter Squadron would become the first operational squadron to fly the Raptor. By then, the 27th formed part of the 1st Fighter Wing, tasked with providing air dominance in defence of the Washington DC Capitol area under Operation Noble Eagle.

The squadron's first F-22A arrived in late 2003 and the squadron continued to grow as more Raptors arrived each month. The 27th FS made the F-22's first flight in support of Operation Noble Eagle in January 2007, and became the first unit to conduct an operational flight with live ordnance loaded in the Raptor.

President George W. Bush established Operation Noble Eagle to protect the American homeland following the terrorist attacks in September 2001.

A depressing interval was provided by the 2013 sequestration when Congress failed to agree on a deficit-reduction, prompting mandatory across-the-board spending cuts and a major reallocation of flying hours. Squadrons either stood down on a rotating basis or were kept combat ready at a reduced readiness level called 'basic mission capable'. The 27th Fighter Squadron suffered a reduction of flying hours, and it was placed into a basic mission capable status from April 5 – September 30, 2013.

The 27th Fighter Squadron became the first to take the Raptor to combat in 2014, during Operation Inherent Resolve (OIR), and during a subsequent OIR deployment in 2017 the squadron celebrated its 100th anniversary. This deployment was in response to the Syrian government's use of chemical weapons, and the threat posed by so-called Islamic State (ISIS). The 27th Fighter Squadron set records for the most bombs dropped by an F-22 squadron in one month, and for the number of GBU-32 JDAMs dropped by an F-22 unit in a single 24 hour period.

Today the 27th Fighter Squadron is a cohesive, combat experienced team that stands ready for any call to support the United States' security requirements.

*The 27th Fighter Squadron 'flagship', with codes presented in a '3D' style, and the Air Combat Command badge. Tail bands are an occasional feature of the F-22 colour scheme, with the 27th using a 'Fightin' Eagles' design. US Air Force*

> **"The 27th Fighter Squadron is the oldest active fighter squadron in the United States Air Force, having amassed more than 100 years of service"**

*Lieutenant Colonel James Hecker delivers the first operational F/A-22 Raptor (03-4042) to its permanent home at Langley Air Force Base, on May 12, 2005. Tail number 3042 was the first of 26 Raptors delivered to the 27th Fighter Squadron – Langley's first Raptor unit. US Air Force, Technical Sergeant Ben Bloker*

# 94th Fighter Squadron

## 'Hat-in-the-Ring Gang'

**THE 94TH FIGHTER SQUADRON** is the second frontline F-22 unit within the 1st Operations Group at Joint Base Langley–Eustis, Virginia. It is one of the oldest units in the United States Air Force, first being organised on August 20, 1917 as the 94th Aero Squadron of the United States Army Air Service at Kelly Field, Texas, with Eddie Rickenbacker among the squadron's most famous members. World War One service led to the unit often being known as the 'Spads' after Rickenbacker's French-built biplane of the same name. During World War Two the unit served in the Mediterranean Theater of Operations (MTO) as part of Twelfth Air Force flying the Lockheed P-38 Lightning. After many years operating in the air defence role, the 94th FS briefly served with TAC, flying the F-4E Phantom from MacDill AFB.

The squadron moved to Langley and re-equipped with the F-15 Eagle in 1976, converting to the F-22 and becoming the USAF's second operational F-22 squadron in 2006. The squadron made its final flight with the F-15 on December 16, 2005.

The 94th received its first F-22A in June 2006, and had picked up its full complement of F-22As by June 2007 with the delivery of 05-0094. This was due to the 94th FS trading its tail number 086 for 094 which had been delivered to the 90th Fighter Squadron, part of the 3rd Wing based at Elmendorf AFB, Alaska. Additional trades included tail number 05-0101, which was traded with the 1st FW for 05-0084. Tail number 10-194 was also used as a flagship by the 94th Fighter Squadron.

The 94th performed the first operational deployment of the F-22 to the CENTCOM area of responsibility in 2011 and have continued to play a part in the air campaign over Iraq and Syria in the fight against the so-called Islamic

State and made the first combat employment of the Small Diameter Bomb from an F-22.

While 2013's sequestration limited flying by the 94th's sister unit, the 94th Fighter Squadron was given a complete stand-down grounding from April 9 - September 30, 2013.

A contingent of 94th Fighter Squadron Airmen and F-22 Raptors assigned to the 1st Fighter Wing, Joint Base Langley-Eustis, Virginia deployed to Andersen Air Force Base, Guam, to conduct missions in the Western Pacific even during the COVID-19 pandemic. Flying operations at Langley never ceased during the pandemic, thereby ensuring the combat readiness of America's most capable fighter wing.

Today, the 94th FS continues the traditions of the Lafayette Escadrille, waiting to face any challenge, anywhere, and carries the spirit of Eddie Rickenbacker and the "Hat-in-the-Ring Gang" into every fight.

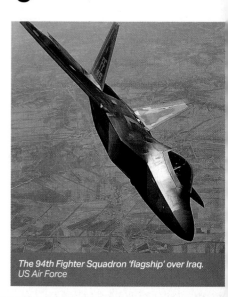

*The 94th Fighter Squadron 'flagship' over Iraq. US Air Force*

*The 94th Fighter Squadron and 94th Fighter Generation Squadron from Joint Base Langley-Eustis, Virginia, broke the record for the most air-to-air missiles loaded and employed by an F-22 Raptor unit during the two-week-long weapons system evaluation programme at Tyndall Air Force Base, Florida, in September 2022. Here the detachment poses in front of 08-4158. US Air Force*

*A US Air Force F-22 Raptor aircraft assigned to the 1st Fighter Wing prepare to take off at Joint Base Langley-Eustis, Virginia, on November 3, 2020. A contingent of 94th Fighter Squadron airmen and F-22s deployed to Andersen Air Force Base, Guam, to conduct missions in the western Pacific with allies and joint partners. US Air Force, Nicholas J. De La Pena*

# 71st Fighter Squadron

## 'Ironmen'

**THE 71ST FIGHTER SQUADRON** has been contributing to the training of F-22 pilots since August 2015, when it reactivated at Langley as the 71st Fighter Training Squadron , flying the Northrop T-38 Talon in the adversary/companion trainer role.

The US Air Force first announced plans to shift F-22 training from Tyndall to Langley in 2019, after the Florida base was hit by Hurricane Michael, which destroyed much of its infrastructure. The decision was taken to rebuild Tyndall as an 'installation of the future' to accommodate a frontline F-35 Wing. To make way for this, the F-22s were moved out.

As an interim step, the F-22 Formal Training Unit, the 43rd Fighter Squadron, was temporarily relocated to Eglin Air Force Base, Florida, though simulators and classroom training remained at Tyndall.

In 2021, the air force approved Langley as the new permanent home of the F-22 FTU pending the completion of an environmental impact study. In June 2023 the air force notified Congress that the environmental impact study was complete, and that 28 F-22s and 16 T-38s would move to Langley, between June and October 2023.

The 71st Fighter Squadron, to which the F-22s and students will now be assigned, had already been reactivated in January (when ACC commander General Mark D. Kelly

> **"In 2021, the air force approved Langley as the new permanent home of the F-22 FTU pending the completion of an environmental impact study."**

*Lieutenant Colonel Andrew Gray, 71st Fighter Squadron commander, prepares to 'deplane' from his F-22 Raptor (02-4040) at Joint Base Langley-Eustis, Virginia, on March 29, 2023. He had arrived from Tyndall AFB as one of the first pair of former 43rd Fighter Squadron aircraft for the new Formal Training Unit. US Air Force, Airman 1st Class Mikaela Smith*

signed a memo formally directing the new schoolhouse to stand up), and on March 29, 2023, the Squadron welcomed its first two F-22 Raptors, (tails AF040 and AF042) to their new home at Joint Base Langley-Eustis. The two aircraft were flown from Tyndall Air Force Base, Florida, by Lieutenant Colonel Andrew Gray, 71st FS commander, and Lieutenant Colonel Matthew Evers, 71st FS director of operations. They were the first of 30 Raptors destined for the 71st FS, the new F-22 Formal Training Unit.

Six US Air Force student pilots (enrolled in the F-22 Basic Flying Course) flew their first F-22 training flights out of Joint Base Langley-Eustis on June 5, 2023, having completed three months of classroom and simulator training at Tyndall. The flying phase at Langley was scheduled to take six months.

Air Combat Command is waiting the completion of a study into tactical aviation requirements, which will determine exactly which and how many tactical aircraft it wants in the fleet moving forward. The air force wants to retire all 32 Block 20 F-22s now used for training, on the grounds that they are too costly to maintain, and because they are not rated for combat, and are increasingly unrepresentative of the frontline F-22 fleet. Congress has specifically prohibited the service from retiring any F-22s until 2027 and there is, as yet no indication that this proviso will be repealed. Until it is, the future of the 71st FS is uncertain.

*Lieutenant Colonel Andrew Gray, 71st Fighter Squadron commander, arrives at Joint Base Langley-Eustis, Virginia in his F-22 Raptor (02-4040), on March 29, 2023. The 43rd Fighter Squadron at Tyndall is winding down as the F-22 Formal Training Unit, with the 71st standing up as the new Raptor 'Schoolhouse'. US Air Force, Airman 1st Class Mikaela Smith*

# 192nd Fighter Wing
## Joint Base Langley-Eustis, Virginia

**THE 192ND WING** (192 WG or 192D Wing), is a unit of the Virginia Air National Guard and the United States Air Force, and is stationed at Joint Base Langley-Eustis, Virginia, co-located with the active duty 1st Fighter Wing. If activated to federal service, the 192nd Wing is gained by Air Combat Command (ACC).

Like all Air National Guard units, the 192nd Wing has a dual mission. The unit's federal mission is one of maintaining a well-trained, well-equipped unit available for prompt mobilisation during war and able to aid during national emergencies (whether natural disasters or civil disturbances). Under its state mission, the 192nd Wing provides protection of life, property and preserves peace, order, and public safety.

In late 2007, following the 2005 BRAC, the 192nd Fighter Wing relinquished its F-16C and F-16D aircraft and moved from Richmond International Airport Air National Guard Station to Langley AFB (now Joint Base Langley-Eustis), to integrate with the regular air force as an associate unit to the 1st Fighter Wing flying the F-22 Raptor.

On October 13, 2007, Lieutenant Colonel Dave Kolmer formally read out the order to reactivate the 192nd Fighter Wing during

Lieutenant Colonel Wade Tolliver, 27th Fighter Squadron Director of Operations, piloting an F-22A Raptor (03-4050) during a training mission off the coast of Virginia, on March 30, 2006. Lieutenant Colonel Bryan Turner and Major Thomas McAtee, both from 149th Fighter Squadron, Virginia Air National Guard, watch the aircraft that their unit would soon be flying from the cockpits of their F-16C Fighting Falcons. US Air Force, Technical Sergeant Ben Bloker

> *"Integration with the active duty 1st Fighter Wing allowed the Air National Guard to be at the forefront of fifth generation fighter aircraft capabilities."*

Three US Air Force F-22 Raptors assigned to the 1st Fighter Wing, Joint Base Langley-Eustis, at the Dubai Air Show, United Arab Emirates, in November 2019. The nearest (10-4192) wears the 'flagship' markings of the 192nd Wing. US Air Force, 2nd Lieutenant Sam Eckholm

Colonel David R. Nardi, 192nd Operations Group commander, delivered the 192nd Fighter Wing's new flagship (tail number 09-4192) to Langley Air Force Base, on March 22, 2012. US National Guard, Master Sergeant Carlos J. Claudio

a ceremony hosted by the 27th Fighter Squadron. Integration with the active duty 1st Fighter Wing allowed the Air National Guard to be at the forefront of fifth generation fighter aircraft capabilities, jointly flying and maintaining the 1st Fighter Wing's F-22 aircraft. Since then, the 192nd Fighter Wing has regularly supported the USAF's mission. In 2017, the wing mobilised for six months to support Operation Inherent Resolve. During this deployment, 534 F-22 Raptor flights were flown, totalling 4,600 combat hours, and dropping 263 bombs on so-called Islamic State targets in Iraq and Syria.

On October 1, 2018, the 192nd Fighter Wing redesignated as the 192nd Wing, reflecting the wing's growth and diversity, which includes a number of competences in addition to F-22 fighter operations and maintenance.

# 149th Fighter Squadron
## Joint Base Langley–Eustis, Virginia

**THE 149TH FIGHTER SQUADRON** is a unit of the Virginia Air National Guard's 192nd Fighter Wing located at Joint Base Langley–Eustis, Virginia. The 149th is the first Air National Guard fighter squadron to fly the F-22 Raptor.

The 149th FS traces its heritage to the 328th Fighter Squadron, the World War Two 'Blue Nose Bastards of Bodney', an 8th Air Force P-51 Mustang unit based at Royal Air Force Bodney, England, which was commanded by Major George Preddy, the leading P-51 ace of the war. As the 149th Fighter Squadron, the Virginia ANG unit was mobilised for the Cuban Missile Crisis and 9/11.

Lieutenant Colonel Phillip Guy became the first VANG pilot to transition to Langley AFB and fly the new F-22A Raptor alongside active duty air force pilots stationed there in October 2005. Lieutenant Colonel Guy and Major Patrick DeConcini flew the first VANG two ship F-22A flight from Langley AFB on February 18, 2006. The 149th FS moved to Langley AFB and transitioned to the F-22 in 2007 as part of a total force integration with Langley's 1st Fighter Wing, and the last Unit Training Assembly was held at the squadron's former base at Richmond in September 2007.

The 192nd FW and its constituent unit, the 149th FS, were reactivated in a ceremony held at the 27th Fighter Squadron, Langley AFB on October 13, 2007. Set-up as a classic 'associate wing' the 192nd FW worked directly with the 1st FW while maintaining its own unit identity and command structure but did not 'own' any of the aircraft.

The 149th was the first Air National Guard squadron to fly the F-22A, marking the first time that the ANG had operated a front-line fighter so soon after it had reached full operational capability. Not everyone was enthusiastic about converting to the new

Major 'Mongo', the 149th Fighter Squadron chief of weapons, won the United States Air Force Instructor Pilot of the Year award for 2017. He is seen here standing in front of the 149th FS flagship F-22 Raptor on November 17, 2017, at Joint Base Langley-Eustis, Virginia. *US Air National Guard, Senior Airman Bryan Myhr*

> **"Not everyone was enthusiastic about converting to the new type and moving to Langley, others didn't like the classic associate arrangement."**

type and moving to Langley, others didn't like the classic associate arrangement, missing the more relaxed atmosphere of the ANG. Some pilots retired, and some sought to join the 121st FS which still flew the F-16 in the nearby DC ANG.

The 149th Fighter Squadron has shouldered its share of deployment activities. Active duty and Virginia National Guard airmen assigned to the 94th Fighter Squadron and 149th Fighter Squadron made a six-month deployment to the Middle East where they were assigned to United States Central Command as part of a theatre security package, providing support and stability to the region. They returned to Langley Air Force Base on October 8, 2015.

Today the unit boasts that pilots from the 149th Fighter Squadron represent: "the most talented collection of combat tested, weapon-school and instructor-pilot qualified citizen airmen in the Air National Guard."

In October 2010, the 192nd Fighter Wing's then flagship (04-4082) was briefly painted with a blue nose to emulate the markings carried by the unit's predecessor 328th Fighter Squadron's P-51 Mustangs - the 'Blue Nosed Bastards of Bodney', and their commander, Major George E. 'Ratsy' Preddy, Jnr who recorded over 26 aerial victories and who named his Mustang *Cripes A'Mighty*. *US Air Force*

# 3rd Wing

## Elmendorf Air Force Base, Alaska

> *The 3rd Wing has grown in size and importance in recent years, thanks to its strategic location."*

Two F-22 Raptors (06-4090 leading 05-4087) fly a training mission near Elmendorf Air Force Base, over rugged Alaskan scenery. The aircraft are assigned to the 3rd Wing at Elmendorf, which is organised as a multi-mission objective wing. Two of the wing's three F-15 units converted to the F-22, the third (the 19th FS) moving to Hawaii to become an active associate unit. US Air Force

**THE 3RD WING** is assigned to the Pacific Air Forces' (PACAF's) Eleventh Air Force, and is stationed at Joint Base Elmendorf-Richardson, Alaska.

The wing is the 11th Air Force's largest unit and its principal component. A composite wing, the 3rd provides air dominance, attack, surveillance, worldwide airlift, and agile combat support forces. The wing's aircraft fly in the air superiority, air interdiction, airborne air surveillance, tactical airlift, theatre resupply, and passenger and troop transport roles.

The mission of the 3rd Wing is to support and defend US interests in the Asia Pacific region and around the world by providing units and aircraft for worldwide air power projection.

As Elmendorf's host unit, the 3rd Wing also maintains the base for forces staging through the base for short-notice US DoD deployments worldwide, maintaining an air base that is capable of meeting United States Pacific Command's theatre staging and throughput requirements. The base also provides medical care for all US forces in Alaska.

The 3rd Wing has grown in size and importance in recent years, thanks to its strategic location and training facilities, and thanks in part to the US 'pivot to the Pacific', though the wing's units and aircraft deployed worldwide – to Europe and Centcom as well as within the PACAF area of responsibility. During 2004, the 3rd Wing fulfilled Air Expeditionary Force (AEF) taskings in support of Operations Enduring Freedom and Iraqi Freedom.

The 3rd Wing began to convert to the F-22A Raptor in 2007, with the 90th Fighter Squadron receiving its first aircraft from August and the wing added a second squadron, the 525th Fighter Squadron to join the 90th in October. The last F-15 assigned to the wing departed in September 2010, marking the end of an era for the wing.

The 302nd Fighter Squadron, assigned to the 477th Fighter Group (Air Force Reserve),

flew 3rd Wing F-22s, and members of that organisation deployed along with their active duty counterparts for the first time in 2010.

The 3rd Wing gave up some aircraft to the 49th Fighter Wing when it stood up with F-22As in 2008, but benefited from the consolidation of the force when Holloman gave up its F-22s and is today one of two frontline fighter wings that fields two frontline Raptor squadrons.

A 3rd Wing F-22 Raptor from Joint Base Elmendorf-Richardson, flies over the Joint Pacific Alaska Range Complex, on July 18, 2019. The JPARC is a 67,000 plus square mile area, providing a realistic training environment giving commanders leverage for full spectrum engagements, ranging from individual skills to complex, large-scale joint engagements. US Air Force, Staff Sergeant James Richardson

# 90th Fighter Squadron

## 'Dicemen'

**THE 90TH FIGHTER SQUADRON** is one of a pair of active duty F-22 squadrons assigned to the 3rd Wing at Joint Base Elmendorf-Richardson, Alaska. The squadron trains in the offensive counter-air (OCA), defensive counter-air (DCA) and suppression of enemy air defences (SEAD) roles, as well as strategic attack and interdiction missions.

The 90th Fighter Squadron began to prepare for significant changes in its mission and weapons system during 2006. Its F-15Es were scheduled to relocate to Mountain Home Air Force Base, Idaho, as part of the BRAC decisions made in 2005. To replace the F-15Es, the 90th began receiving the advanced F-22 Raptor in August 2007. Its first aircraft, and the first of 40 F-22A Raptors at Elmendorf AFB was the first F-22A to be permanently based outside the contiguous United States.

Twelve F-22 Raptor aircraft assigned to the 90th Fighter Squadron at Joint Base Elmendorf-Richardson, Alaska, forward deployed to the 32nd Tactical Air Base at Łask, Poland, on August 4, 2022, to support NATO Air Shielding, operating as the 90th Expeditionary Fighter Squadron. The F-22As (which arrived carrying ferry tanks) took over the air policing mission from the F-16Cs of the Vermont Air National Guard's 158th Fighter Wing, which had arrived in theatre on May 2, 2022, and which had operated from Spangdahlem Air Base, Germany during their three-month rotational deployment.

The NATO Air Shielding mission is an enhanced posture that integrates Allied air and surface based air and missile defence while offering a range of rapidly deployable options from the Baltic to the Black seas and providing the flexibility necessary to address any emerging threat in the region.

The F-22 deployment at Łask also supported USAF Agile Combat Employment

*Lieutenant Colonel Joseph Kunkel, commander of the 90th Fighter Squadron, seen after dismounting from F-22 Raptor 09-4190 on March 7, 2012. The 90th Fighter Squadron was previously equipped with the F-15E Strike Eagle, before re-equipping with the Raptor. US Air Force, Steve White*

operations throughout the region, helping to validate new ways of deploying assets during a crisis or conflict in order to operate in contested environments. The F-22 demonstrated the ability to move across the theatre to present layers of operational unpredictability and to complicate an adversary's strategic decision making.

Lieutenant Colonel Michael Kendall, 90th EFS commander said that: "The air force has relied on F-22 deployments to improve combined tactical air operations, enhance interoperability of forces, and deter potential threats for the past 15 years. Raptor capabilities allow us to provide air superiority and dominance, rapidly and at great distances. We came here to enhance NATO's posture and increase warfighting capabilities along the eastern flank in support of our allies and partners. The F-22 ensures a lethality that no other aircraft can provide. We are unwavering in our commitment to extended deterrence and ready to go whenever they need us."

*Lieutenant Colonel Nicholas Reed taxiing in the squadron flagship (09-4190), laden with external fuel tanks ready for a long ferry flight to Andersen AFB on the island of Guam. US Air Force*

**"The F-22As took over the air policing mission from the F-16Cs of the Vermont Air National Guard's 158th Fighter Wing."**

*Twelve 90th Fighter Squadron F-22 Raptor aircraft from Joint Base Elmendorf-Richardson, Alaska, forward deployed to the 32nd Tactical Air Base, Łask, Poland, to support NATO Air Shielding, from August 4, 2022. Valdimir Putin's illegal invasion of Ukraine in February 2022 has seen a massive uplift in NATO air defence and deterrent activity, especially in the Baltic States, Poland, and Romania. US Air Force, Staff Sergeant Danielle Sukhlall*

# 525th Fighter Squadron

## 'Bulldogs'

**THE 525TH FIGHTER SQUADRON** is today equipped with the Lockheed Martin F-22 Raptor and was the second active duty Raptor unit to form at Elmendorf. It did so after a long period of inactivity, despite an impressive history, most recently as a USAFE fighter squadron.

The 525th deployed to Incirlik Air Base, Turkey, in December 1990 with its F-15C Eagles, where it formed part of the 7440th Combat Wing (Provisional) The squadron flew 1,329 combat sorties totalling 3,550 combat hours during Operations Desert Shield and Desert Storm. The squadron shot down six enemy aircraft without loss, returning to Bitburg AFB, Germany, on 13 March 1991. The 525th inactivated at Bitburg, its home for 35 years, on April 1, 1992.

After 15 years, Pacific Air Forces activated the 525th Fighter Squadron as the second active-duty F-22 Raptor squadron within the 3rd Wing at Elmendorf Air Force Base, Alaska, on October 29, 2007, nearly three months after its first aircraft officially landed at Elmendorf. Lieutenant Colonel Chuck Corcoran assumed command of the squadron, with an initial cadre of five pilots and four support staff.

Colonel Corcoran said at the time that: "Our job is to clear the skies of enemy aircraft, as well as take out any surface-to-air missiles that would deny us access to enemy airspace. The overarching reason for that is to gain control of the skies. That's what the F-22 was built to do and it's our mission here at Elmendorf."

In fact, the 525th trains in the fighter missions of offensive and defensive counterair (air-to-air), but also strategic attack, interdiction, offensive counterair (air-to-surface), suppression of enemy air defences, and the precision engagement of surface targets using a wide variety of conventional air-to-surface munitions.

The 525th received the very last F-22 built for the Air Force (Raptor 4195), which arrived

The 525th Fighter Squadron received this aircraft (10-4195), the last Raptor off the line in 2012, and used it as the unit's 'flagship'. US Air Force chief of staff General Norman A. Schwartz handed over a symbolic 'key' to the last production F-22 Raptor to Lieutenant Colonel Paul Moga, 525th Fighter Squadron commander and his crew chief, Staff Sergeant Damon Crawford, at the Lockheed Martin Aeronautics Company factory at Marietta, Georgia on May 2, 2012. US Air Force

> ## "The 525th inactivated at Bitburg, its home for 35 years, on April 1, 1992."

The previous 525th Fighter Squadron flagship (06-4125) was one of 14 Raptors from Elmendorf Air Force Base, Alaska forced to 'bed down' at Holloman Air Force Base, in February 2009 after volcanic activity was observed at Mount Redoubt near Elmendorf. The Raptor's thrust vectoring 'paddles' can clearly be seen in this view. US Air Force, Technical Sergeant Chris Flahive

Lieutenant Colonel Brandon Tellez (who is, in 2023, the commander of the 1st Fighter Wing) became the 23rd pilot to reach 1,000 flying hours in a Raptor on June 22, 2016. At the time, Tellez was the CO of the 525th Fighter Squadron. US Air Force, Airman 1st Class Javier Alvarez

at JB Elmendorf-Richardson, Alaska, on May 5, 2012, completing the bed down of the Raptor fleet. Lieutenant Colonel Paul Moga, the then-commander of the 525th Fighter Squadron, flew the aircraft on its eight-hour, non-stop ferry flight from Lockheed Martin's production facility in Marietta, Georgia. "It's good to have this jet where it belongs," said Moga, who went on to fly the aircraft as the squadron's flagship.

Most recently, the 525th Expeditionary Fighter Squadron deployed to Kadena Air Base, Japan, for a five-month deployment to support Pacific Air Forces' efforts to bring more advanced fighter aircraft forward to the western Pacific while Kadena Air Base's own F-15C Eagles began their journey back to the United States. The squadron returned to Alaska on April 8, 2023 having flown 1,100 sorties, integrating with both joint and ally and partner nation air force forces and while simultaneously supporting Operations Iron Shadow and Iron Express, Exercise Agile Reaper 23-1, and the USAF F-22 demonstration team at the Avalon Australia International Trade Show.

The squadron also showcased the F-22 Raptor on the Korean Peninsula for the first time in five years, and for the first time ever in the Philippines and Tinian, Commonwealth of the Northern Mariana Islands.

# 477th Fighter Group

**THE 477TH FIGHTER GROUP** was Air Force Reserve Command's first F-22A Raptor unit but had its origins as the 477th Bombardment Group. This was originally established in May 1943 as a Bombardment Group to train those Tuskegee airmen destined to become bomber aircrew.

The 477th Fighter Group is a classic associate unit responsible for recruiting, training, developing, and retaining reserve citizen airmen to support the 3rd Wing and

Expeditionary Air Force mission requirements. The active duty (regular) component unit retains principal responsibility for the Wing's F-22s, but it shares this with the 477th FG as its reserve component unit. The active and reserve component units retain separate organisational structures and chains-of-command.

The men and women of the 477th FG are integrated with the active duty Air Force 3rd Wing, as partners in most F-22A mission

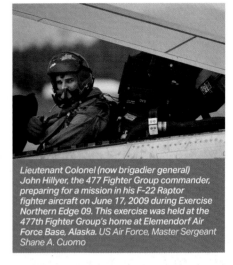

*Lieutenant Colonel (now brigadier general) John Hillyer, the 477 Fighter Group commander, preparing for a mission in his F-22 Raptor fighter aircraft on June 17, 2009 during Exercise Northern Edge 09. This exercise was held at the 477th Fighter Group's home at Elmendorf Air Force Base, Alaska. US Air Force, Master Sergeant Shane A. Cuomo*

*Raptors arriving at RAAF Base Tindal in February 2017 for an Enhanced Air Cooperation Initiative exercise. This aircraft wears 477th Fighter Group markings. US Air Force, Staff Sergeant Alexander Martinez*

areas and provides a combat-ready force of approximately 300 air reserve technicians, traditional reservists, and civil servants assigned to operations, maintenance, medical and mission support units. They increase the wing's efficiency and overall combat capability while retaining reserve administrative support and career enhancement.

The 477th FG leverages the traditional reserve component strengths of experience and continuity to fly, and fight, and win as unrivalled wingmen on the total force team at Joint Base Elmendorf-Richardson, operating what they claim is "the world's most capable fighter aircraft."

# 302nd Fighter Squadron 'Hellions'

**THE 302ND FIGHTER SQUADRON** is part of the Air Force Reserve Command's 477th Fighter Group at Elmendorf Air Force Base, Alaska. It operates the F-22 primarily in the air dominance/ air superiority role.

The 302nd Fighter Squadron had its origins as one of the four African-American fighter squadrons of the 332nd Fighter Group (the Tuskegee Airmen) which saw combat during World War Two in the European and Mediterranean theatres of operations from February 17, 1944 to 20 February 20, 1945. From 1956 to 1974 the squadron was an

Air Force Reserve search and rescue unit, transferring to the fighter role in 1987, after a stint as a combat search and rescue unit.

In 2007, the squadron relocated from Luke AFB to Elmendorf and transitioned from the F-16 Fighting Falcon to the F-22 Raptor, which it continues to operate as an Associate AFRC unit with the active duty Air Force's 3rd Wing.

Lieutenant Colonel David Piffarerio, 302nd Fighter Squadron commander, flew his 1,000th flight hour in the F-22 Raptor on November 4th, 2011, becoming the first US Air Force pilot to do so.

*Lieutenant Colonel Ryan Pelkola, the 302nd Fighter Squadron director of operations, clocked up 2,000 flying hours on August 7, 2021 at Joint Base Elmendorf-Richardson, Alaska. Pelkola was the first F-22 Raptor pilot to reach this milestone, which for him took 14 years and 1,323 sorties to achieve. US Air Force, Staff Sergeant Melissa Estevez*

*An F-22 Raptor flies above Anchorage during a routine training mission. This F-22 represents Air Force Reserve Command's first F-22 Associate Unit located at Elmendorf Air Force Base, Alaska. The 302nd Fighter Squadron stood up in October 2007 and belongs to the 477th Fighter Group. US Air Force, Technical Sergeant Keith Brown*

# 15th Wing

## Hickam Air Force Base, Hawaii

**THE 15TH WING AT** Hickam AFB, on the island of O'ahu in the State of Hawaii, reports to PACAF's 11th Air Force, Headquartered at Joint Base Elmendorf-Richardson, Alaska. Hickam AFB merged with Naval Station Pearl Harbor in 2010 to become part of the newly formed Joint Base Pearl Harbor–Hickam.

Hickam has a long history, most notably for being heavily attacked when the Imperial Japanese Navy's aircraft attacked O'ahu on December 7, 1941 to eliminate air opposition and to prevent American aircraft from following them back to their aircraft carriers. Hickam suffered extensive damage, aircraft losses, and casualties including 189 personnel killed and 303 wounded.

The 15th Airlift Wing was redesignated as the 15th Wing on May 18, 2010, in anticipation of the addition of air refuelling and fighters to its core airlift mission. In October 2010, the wing added Lockheed Martin F-22 Raptors to its roster when the 19th Fighter Squadron moved from Joint Base Elmendorf-Richardson, Alaska to become an active duty associate unit of the Hawaiian Air National Guard's 199th Fighter Squadron.

The first two of 20 F-22 Raptors were formally dedicated at a Joint Base Pearl Harbor-Hickam ceremony on Friday, July 9, 2010. The ceremony marked the beginning of the partnership between the Hawaii Air National Guard and the active duty air force flying the fifth generation F-22. The Raptors are flown by pilots from the 199th Fighter Squadron, 154th Wing, Hawaii Air National Guard and by active duty air force pilots from the 19th Fighter Squadron, 15th Wing. A combination of Hawaii Air National Guardsmen and active duty airmen maintain them.

The mission of the 15th Wing is to develop and sustain combat-ready airmen, in partnership with the total force, to provide global mobility, global reach, precision engagement, and agile combat support, partnering with the 154th Wing of the Hawaii Air National Guard.

Two 15th Wing F-22As (04-4079 and 05-4084) in flight over the GABA (Great Australian Bugger All) during a deployment to Australia to take part in Exercise Talisman Sabre, 2023. The deployed unit was named the 199th Air Expeditionary Squadron and included personnel from the active duty 15th Wing's 19th Fighter Squadron, and Guard personnel from the 199th Fighter Squadron, 154th Wing, Hawaii Air National Guard. *Royal Australian Air Force*

# 19th Fighter Squadron

**THE 19TH FIGHTER SQUADRON** forms part of the Pacific Air Forces' (PACAF) 15th Wing based at Joint Base Pearl Harbor–Hickam, Hawaii.

The squadron is one of the oldest in the United States Air Force, its origins dating to June 14, 1917, and it served overseas in France as part of the American Expeditionary Force during World War One. The squadron saw combat during World War Two and became part of the Tactical Air Command during the Cold War.

Located in Alaska at Joint Base Elmendorf-Richardson since January 1, 1994 the 19th Fighter Squadron relocated to Joint Base Pearl Harbor-Hickam and transitioned to the Lockheed-Martin F-22 Raptor from the McDonnell-Douglas F-15C/D. In the process, the 19th FS became the first active duty associate unit flying the Raptor.

Today the 19th FS operates the F-22 Raptor conducting offensive and defensive counterair (air-to-air) as well as strategic attack, interdiction, and SEAD (suppression of enemy air defences) missions.

The squadron has practised dynamic force employment, making short notice deployments to operate from unpredictable locations. In March-April 2021, for example, the squadron forward deployed to MCAS-Iwakuni in Japan for almost a month to train with Japanese and US Marine Corps aircraft. The F-22s were co-located with USMC F-35Bs, allowing them to practice joint integration between the two fifth generation fighters.

An HH-coded F-22 aircraft takes off from Nellis Air Force Base to participate in an Exercise Red Flag 19-1 mission. The 19th Fighter Squadron has no aircraft of its own, operating as an associate unit to the ANG 154th Wing. As such, HH tail codes are augmented by the Minuteman badge of the Guard. *Royal Australian Air Force*

# 154th Wing

## Hickam Air Force Base, Hawaii

**THE 154TH WING IS** the major operational component of the Hawaii Air National Guard, stationed at Hickam Air Force Base, Joint Base Pearl Harbor–Hickam, Honolulu, Hawaii. The Hawaii ANG has a state mission, providing organised, trained units to protect Hawaii's citizens and property, preserve peace, and ensure public safety in response to natural or human-caused disasters.

Its federal mission is to provide operationally ready combat units, combat support units, and qualified personnel for active duty in the US Air Force in time of war, national emergency, or operational contingency. If activated to federal service, the wing would be placed under the command of the Pacific Air Forces (PACAF).

The 154th Wing is a composite wing, consisting of Air Supremacy, Airlift, Radar, and Air Refuelling squadrons, and in certain instances functions as an associate unit with the USAF Pacific Air Forces' 15th Wing.

The Hawaii Air National Guard received the first of its 20 F-22A Raptors In July 2010, the initial aircraft being transferred from the 325th Fighter Wing, at Tyndall. The

*A USAF F-22 Raptor arrives at RAAF Base Tindal in Australia's Northern Territory as part of the Enhanced Air Cooperation Initiative which forms part of the Force Posture Agreement between the United States and Australia. The 154th is both a composite wing, consisting of Air Supremacy, Airlift, Radar, and Air Refuelling squadrons, and also an associate unit with the USAF Pacific Air Forces' 15th Wing. Royal Australian Air Force*

remaining 18 aircraft were transferred from the 1st Fighter Wing, at Langley. The last F-15 left in 2011.

The 154th Wing was the second ANG unit to be equipped with the F-22.

The Hawaii ANG's 199th Fighter Squadron operates alongside the active-duty 19th

Fighter Squadron as an associate unit, although the Guard is responsible for 75% of the mission configuration. This was the first time an Air National Guard unit had taken the position of lead squadron in an associate flying unit arrangement with the active duty air force.

# 199th Fighter Squadron

The 199th Fighter Squadron (199th FS) is a unit of the Hawaii Air National Guard's 154th Wing located at Joint Base Pearl Harbor–Hickam, Honolulu, Hawaii. The 199th is equipped with the F-22A Raptor.

The Hawaii Air National Guard received the first of its new F-22s in July 2010, becoming

the second ANG unit to be so equipped. The initial pair of aircraft were transferred from the 325th Fighter Wing, the other 18 aircraft coming from the 1st Fighter Wing.

The 199th operates with the active-duty 19th Fighter Squadron as their cadre unit, although the Hawaii ANG is responsible for 75% of the

mission configuration. This is the first time that an Air National Guard unit has had an active duty squadron as its cadre flying unit.

The 199th Fighter Squadron thereby acts as a reverse associate to the active duty 19th Fighter Squadron. Together the two units form the Hawaiian Raptors.

*Raptors from the 199th Fighter Squadron fly alongside a US Air Force KC-135 Stratotanker from the 909th Air Refueling Squadron during 5th generation fighter training near Mount Fuji, Japan, on April 1, 2021. The F-22 Raptors were operating out of Marine Corps Air Station Iwakuni, Japan, to support PACOM's dynamic force employment concept. The 199th operates with the active-duty 19th Fighter Squadron as their cadre unit, although the Hawaii ANG is responsible for 75% of the mission configuration. This is the first time an Air National Guard unit has had an active duty squadron as a cadre flying unit, rather than vice versa. US Air Force, Senior Airman Rebeckah Medeiros*

# Test Raptors

On a rare rainy day in the Mojave Desert during October 2003, the F-22 Combined Test Force put Raptor 4001 through wet-runway testing at speeds of 30, 60 and 90kts. 91-4001 was the first of nine Engineering, Manufacture, and Development Raptors. It was grounded permanently on November 2, 2000 and was then used for live-fire/battle damage survivability tests. US Air Force, Kevin Robertson

**US AIR FORCE F-22** testing goes back to the first days of the ATF fly-off, with the Lockheed- and Northrop-led YF-22 and YF-23 teams sharing a hangar at Edwards AFB, and operating under the auspices of the 6511th Test Squadron.

The 6511th then tested the YF-22 second prototype until its loss in April 1992. The Squadron was redesignated the 411th Test Squadron in October 1992 and then planned for the F-22 test programme, receiving the first Lockheed Martin F-22A Raptor in February 1998.

Today, F-22 test and evaluation duties are shared between two commands. Air Force

Materiel Command (AFMC) is responsible for development testing (DT&E) and also for Initial Operational Test and Evaluation. Like Air Force Systems Command before it, AFMC is responsible for the testing conducted at Edwards AFB.

Air Combat Command is responsible for testing new operational capabilities (OT&E) and for evaluating fielded capabilities, its test activities co-ordinated by the the United States Air Force Warfare Center at Nellis Air Force Base. Nellis is the home of the 57th Wing, with the USAF Weapons School and the 433rd Weapons Squadron. Nellis is also home to the 59th TES

and 422nd TES, though these geographically separated units notionally belong to the 53rd Wing based at far-off Eglin AFB in Florida!

F-22 testing has sometimes included some unexpected experiments. In March 2011, the 411th FLTS successfully flew the F-22 with a 50/50 fuel blend of conventional JP-8 and a biofuel. More recently, In September 2022, an F-22 flew with onboard software developed by a third party, and subsequently flew a software application that was then tested on an F-35 – the first time that the same software has been used on both types, according to the USAF's 412th Test Wing.

The 411th Flight Test Squadron dwindled to four F-22As (91-4004, 91-4007, 91-4009, and 06-4132) by 2015, after having had nine aircraft at one stage. But in the summer of 2016, the squadron was reinforced by four operational F-22s from Langley (04-4073 and 08-4170), Nellis (06-4109) and Tyndall (05-4084). US Air Force, Christian Turner

# 53rd Test and Evaluation Group
## Nellis Air Force Base, Nevada

**THE 53RD TEST AND** Evaluation Group is part of the 53rd Wing at Eglin AFB in Florida, but is itself headquartered at Nellis AFB, Nevada, and reports to the United States Air Force Warfare Center on the site, a direct reporting unit to Headquarters Air Combat Command.

The 53rd Wing serves as the focal point for the Combat Air Forces and is tasked with testing new operational capabilities and evaluating fielded capabilities. The unit claims to 'perfect lethality' and 'bring the future faster' by answering warfighter demands for integrated, multi-domain capabilities, giving them the latest safe and effective hardware, software, weapons and tactics techniques, and procedures to win America's wars.

The 53rd Wing's three groups employ more than 1,600 airmen and operate some 25 distinct platforms from 16 geographically separated locations throughout the US.

The 53rd Test and Evaluation Group (TEG) manages and executes Air Combat Command's operational test and evaluation and tactics development for the 'big five' tactical aircraft platforms (A-10, F-15C/E/EX, F-16, F-35, and F-22) and for the MQ-9 Reaper, HH-60G/W Pave Hawk, HC-130J Combat King II, and EC-130 Compass Call weapons systems. The group also supports foreign military exploitation and advanced technology demonstrations, and manages the evaluation of all air-to-air and air-to-ground weapons, mission planning systems, electronic warfare systems, aircrew flight equipment and agile combat support systems.

*The 53rd TEG 'flagship' (09-4188) takes off from Nellis Air Force Base, Nevada, on June 15, 2023. The unit's aircraft use an 'OT' (Operational Test) tail code. US Air Force, William R. Lewis*

The 53rd Test and Evaluation Group was activated on November 20, 1998 through the re-designation of the 4443rd Test and Evaluation Group and moved from Eglin AFB to Nellis AFB In 1999.

The group consists of seven squadrons, two direct detachments, and a named flight and performs tactical development, operational tests, and evaluations for Air Combat Command.

Air Force Secretary Frank Kendall has said that the F-22 will be the USAF's air dominance solution until the Next-Generation Air Dominance [NGAD] enters service. With a rapidly evolving threat F-22 modernisation is vital, and the 53rd Test and Evaluation Group is at the very heart of the Raptor Agile Capability Release (RACR) enhancement programme.

# 59th Test and Evaluation Squadron

**THE 59TH TEST AND** Evaluation Squadron is assigned to the 53rd Test Management Group at Nellis AFB, Nevada which formed a geographically separated element of Air Combat Command's 53rd Wing at Eglin. The squadron has served at Nellis for test and evaluation since December 2004. It does not have assigned aircraft.

The 59th Test and Evaluation Squadron is responsible for the management of A-10, F-15C/E, F-16, F-22, HH-60, and Guardian Angel weapon system testing including force development evaluations, tactics development and evaluations, and software evaluations. Squadron personnel direct operational test planning and execution, as well as data gathering, analysing, and reporting for the above systems operated by the CAF. The squadron also manages the OT&E of weapons and support systems in order to improve current and future combat capabilities.

*An F-22 Raptor assigned to the 422nd Test and Evaluation Squadron takes off for a training mission from Nellis Air Force Base, Nevada, on January 7, 2021. US Air Force, William R. Lewis*

# 422nd Test and Evaluation Squadron

## 'Green Bats'

**THE 422ND TEST AND** Evaluation Squadron is a geographically separated unit of the 53rd Wing, based at Eglin Air Force Base, Florida, but forms part of the 53rd Test and Evaluation Group, at Nellis Air Force Base, Nevada. The squadron performs operational testing of all fighter aircraft and munitions entering service or in operational use by Air Combat Command and as such is claimed to be the most diverse-equipped aircraft squadron in the United States Air Force. The composite squadron currently includes examples of the A-10 Thunderbolt II, McDonnell Douglas F-15C Eagle, McDonnell Douglas F-15E Strike Eagle, General Dynamics F-16 Fighting Falcon, and Lockheed Martin F-35 Lightning II, operating within type-specific 'Divisions'.

The squadron was reactivated in 1969, by re-designating the 4539th Fighter Weapons Squadron at Nellis Air Force Base, Nevada, as the 422d Fighter Weapons Squadron. The 422

Fighter Weapons Squadron's name changed to the 422d Test and Evaluation Squadron (TES) in 1982, to better reflect its role.

On October 1, 1996, the 422nd TES was realigned under the 53rd Wing at Eglin Air Force Base, Florida, when the United States Air Warfare Center assigned all testing to the 53rd Wing. The squadron grew when it inherited all test management, advanced programmes, and test support from the 57th Test Group.

Today the squadron is a Nellis-based Tactical Air Command operational evaluation unit, providing combat evaluation and operational testing of new USAF aircraft, engines, software, and weapons upgrades entering the inventory after developmental testing has been completed at Edwards Air Force Base or at Eglin.

After a new fighter weapons system or sub-system or upgrade completes

developmental testing at Edwards or Eglin, the 422nd TES is tasked with thoroughly vetting the new equipment in a combat representative environment.

In addition to its operational testing mandate, the 422d TES is also responsible for the development and testing of new tactics for the USAF, including tactics intended to counter new and emerging threat systems. The squadron works closely with the USAF Weapons School, and also supports foreign materiel exploitation.

The squadron's F-22 division was established in 2004 for testing and evaluation of the F-22A Raptor, though the first production aircraft had been delivered to Edwards AFB for IOT&E in October 2002, joining the 422nd TES in January 2003.

IOT&E began on April 29, 2004 and was completed in December 2004. Five different F/A-22s were flown during the operational

This US Air Force (USAF) F/A-22 Raptor (PRTV aircraft 4013) was being flown by Major David Thole of the 422nd Test and Evaluation Squadron (TES), at Nellis Air Force Base when photographed in 2004. The F-16 alongside was being flown by the then-major Alex Grynkewich of the 53rd Test and Evaluation Group (TEG). Today, the latter is Lieutenant General Alexus G. Grynkewich, commander of the Ninth Air Force, while Thole retired a Lieutenant Colonel! US Air Force

An F-22 Raptor (04-4068) assigned to the 422nd Test and Evaluation Squadron (TES), takes off for a mission at Nellis Air Force Base, Nevada, on January 12, 2021. The 422nd TES is a geographically separated unit of the 53rd Test and Evaluation Group, at Eglin AFB, Florida. US Air Force, William R. Lewis

> ## "The mission of the 422nd Test and Evaluation Squadron continues to grow in scope and complexity as new aircraft and systems are developed for use in the combat air forces."

effectiveness testing portion of the F/A-22 IOT&E, with up to four F/A-22s participating in a variety of simulated combat scenarios. Seven USAF pilots flew the Raptor in the IOT&E missions at Edwards AFB, including Lieutenant Colonel Art McGettrick, commander of the 422nd TES, and Major Alexus Grynkewich, chief of F/A-22 standards evaluation at the 422nd TES.

Nellis carried out the first complete mission demonstration of the Raptor's air-to-ground capability using JDAM (and aircraft 00-4016) on September 2, 2004, and Follow On OT&E for the air-to-ground role was undertaken the next year. The software required to drop JDAM, not available for IOT&E, was loaded onto the Raptors of the 422nd in early 2005.

The mission of the 422nd Test and Evaluation Squadron continues to grow in scope and complexity as new aircraft and systems are developed for use in the combat air forces.

The squadrons aircraft wear an 'OT' (Operational Test) tail code, usually with a green/black checkerboard tail flash, though on the F-22s this was presented in a toned down 'grey-on-grey' form.

The 422nd Test and Evaluation Squadron and the 59th Test Squadron conducted the first in-flight vapor purge tests on the F-22 Raptor from October 13-21, 2022. These tests were a continuation of the Next Generation Aircrew Protection (NGAP) programme and aimed to evaluate the time it took to clear the cockpit of a simulated chemical agent during flight. Methyl salicylate, also known as wintergreen oil, and widely used as flavouring agent in chewing gums and mints was sprayed into the aircraft's engines before take-off and then the concentration of the chemical during flight was measured to measure the speed at which a contaminant was purged from the cockpit.

# 57th Wing
## Nellis Air Force Base, Nevada

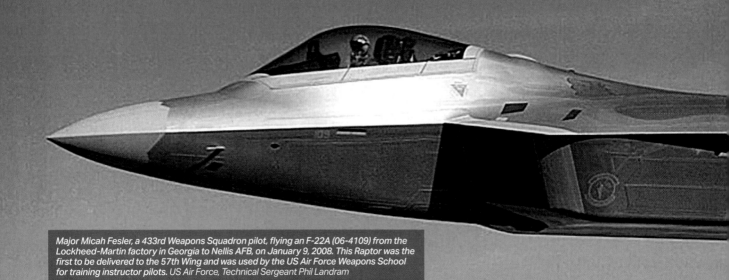

Major Micah Fesler, a 433rd Weapons Squadron pilot, flying an F-22A (06-4109) from the Lockheed-Martin factory in Georgia to Nellis AFB, on January 9, 2008. This Raptor was the first to be delivered to the 57th Wing and was used by the US Air Force Weapons School for training instructor pilots. *US Air Force, Technical Sergeant Phil Landram*

**THE 57TH WING (57** WG) is an operational component of the United States Air Force (USAF) Warfare Center, based at Nellis Air Force Base, Nevada and reporting to Air Combat Command. The 57th Wing formed in October 1969 by redesignating the 4525th Fighter Weapons Wing at Nellis Air Force Base and assumed operational control of 'Red Flag' exercises in October 1979. The wing was reorganised in 2005 to reflect its current structure.

The 57th Wing claims to be 'the most diverse wing in the Air Force' and is the home to advanced air combat training in the US Air Force. It also conducts operational tests and evaluations, demonstrates tactical fighter weapon systems, and develops fighter tactics. The wing is tasked with providing realistic, advanced, and multi-domain training focused on ensuring dominance through air, space, and cyberspace, training composite strike forces which can include every type of aircraft in the USAF inventory. Training is conducted in conjunction with air and ground units of the US Army, US Navy, US Marine Corps, and air forces from allied nations, and incorporates adversary tactics, dissimilar air combat training, and electronic warfare.

Aircrew do not come to the 57th Wing in order to learn how to fly, but instead to learn how to be combat aviators. The wing aims to achieve this by training and preparing innovative leaders in high-end warfighting, and by ensuring that the USAF's combat air forces are well trained and well equipped and ready to deploy into a combat theatre to conduct integrated combat operations. Their alumni are "prepared for tomorrow's victories," according to the unit's own website!

The 57th Wing includes the United States Air Force Weapons School, the 57th Operations Group (which consists of

Aggressor squadrons that replicate adversary threat tactics), and even the USAF Aerial Demonstration Squadron (the Thunderbirds).

## GRADUATES

The US Air Force Weapons School provides graduate-level instructor courses that provide advanced training in weapons and tactics employment to officers from the Combat Air Forces, Mobility Air Forces and Space Forces. Every six months, the school produces approximately 130 graduates who return to their units as weapons and tactics officers - expert instructors on weapons, weapons systems, and air, space and cyberspace integration providing advanced instruction and battlefield guidance to their commanders, operations officers, and colleagues.

United States Air Force Weapons School students are fully qualified instructors, chosen by a central selection board, from the best of their peer groups. Students receive an average of 400 hours of academic instruction and participate in demanding combat training missions in their respective aircraft. The course culminates in the three-week Advanced Integration phase, in which students demonstrate their ability to effectively employ and integrate multiple weapons systems to

defeat complex peer-level adversaries in a staged battle over the Nevada Test and Training Range.

The Weapons School consists of 21 Weapons Squadrons (WPS) and eight Advanced Instructor Courses (AIC). These are based at nine locations across the country. Thirteen squadrons are based at Nellis Air Force Base, with eight geographically separated units at Hurlburt Field, Florida, Little Rock AFB, Arkansas, and Rosecrans ANGB, Joint Base Lewis-McChord, Washington, Dyess AFB, Texas, Whiteman AFB, Missouri, Barksdale AFB, Louisiana, and Fairchild AFB, Washington.

Several of the Nellis-based squadrons do not operate aircraft, instead training cyber, space, and even ICBM instructors. Those that do include the 6th WPS (F-35A), the 16th WPS (F-16), the 17th WPS (F-15E), the 66th WPS (A-10C and JTAC training), and the 433rd WPS, which is responsible for F-22 training.

Aircraft assigned to the 57th Operations Group and Weapons School wear the tail code 'WA'. This dates back to the days when Las Vegas Air Force Base used the code 'WA' in homage to Western Airlines and "the advancement of aviation in the southwestern United States."

> *"Students receive an average of 400 hours of academic instruction and participate in demanding combat training missions in their respective aircraft."*

The same aircraft heads a lineup of Raptors at Edwards AFB in 2016. On October 30, 2020, this F-22A, experienced an overheat condition in the auxiliary power unit exhaust bay that resulted in $2.69m in damages to the airframe. *US Air Force, Christian Turner*

# 433rd Weapons Squadron

## 'Satan's Angels'

**THE 433RD WEAPONS SQUADRON** is assigned to the USAF Weapons School at Nellis AFB, Nevada, forming part of the 57th Wing. The squadron carries the informal nickname 'Satan's Angels', and its aircraft carry 'WA' tail codes and black/yellow checkerboard fin stripes, though the latter are toned down on the F-22 and appear as two shades of grey.

The 433rd Weapons Squadron reactivated as part of the 57th Fighter Weapons Wing at Nellis AFB, Nevada on October 1, 1976 to test and evaluate systems modifications to the McDonnell Douglas F-15A Eagle. That mission was subsequently assumed by the USAF Fighter Weapons School F-15 Division and the squadron inactivated on December 30, 1976.

The squadron reactivated at Nellis AFB in February 2003, replacing the USAF Fighter Weapons School F-15C Division. Its new mission was to conduct Weapons Instructors Courses at the USAF Weapons School and to provide advanced training in weapons and tactics employment. Graduates would then return to their units, where they would train their colleagues in the latest tactics, techniques, and procedures.

The squadron received its first F-22 Raptor on January 9, 2008, when Major Micah Fesler, a 433rd Weapons Squadron pilot and Virginia Air National Guardsman, delivered the 57th Wing's first F-22A, the first of six Raptors planned to be delivered to the 433rd Weapons Squadron by September 2008. The aircraft was delivered direct from the Lockheed-Martin factory in Marietta, Georgia.

"Flying that F-22 was exciting because I literally picked it up from the factory," Maj Fesler later remembered. With the arrival of the Raptors, the 433rd Weapons Squadron found itself flying both fourth-generation and fifth-generation fighter aircraft – which Fesler described as "a huge step for the integration of air dominance assets."

Between the delivery of the first aircraft and January 2009, squadron members began developing the course material – a significant task, bearing in mind the requirement for some 360 hours of academics. The entire syllabus had to be designed in detail, and every sortie had to be planned, together with briefings for every sortie.

"It is a fairly large undertaking because we are starting with a blank slate," Fesler said.

Lieutenant Colonel Pete Milohnic, 433rd Weapons Squadron commander said that the process of standing up the F-22A Weapons School course had to be a collaborative

*An F-22 Raptor and F-15 Eagle from the US Air Force Weapons School, the 433rd Weapons Squadron, at Nellis Air Force Base, Nevada, flying in formation over Lake Mead, on July 16, 2010. The Weapons School teaches graduate-level weapons and tactics instructor courses. US Air Force, Master Sergeant Kevin J. Gruenwald*

> **"With the arrival of the Raptors, the 433rd Weapons Squadron found itself flying both fourth-generation and fifth-generation fighter aircraft."**

An F-22 Raptor assigned to the 433rd Weapons Squadron at Nellis Air Force Base, Nevada, banks, and fires flares as it flies over the Nevada Test and Training Range on July 10, 2017. *US Air Force, Staff Sergeant Daryn Murphy*

Gary Rose, at the time, the 433rd Weapons Squadron assistant director of operations. "It is the future of the air force."

Despite the changes, the 433rd WPS claims to have "held fast to the tradition of producing the world's greatest air supremacy pilots." The squadron has a strong heritage of success to live up to. Since the squadron began producing F-15 weapons officers, the F-15s have maintained an undefeated, 104-0 kill-to-loss record, and 12 F-15C Weapons School graduates accounted for 18 of the USAF's 38 F-15C air-to-air victories.

By April 2017, the 433rd WPS had graduated 524 Air Dominance patch wearers, consisting of 482 F-15C and 42 F-22 pilots.

The F-15C Eagles were officially retired shortly following WSINT 21B in December of 2021, leaving the unit as an all-Raptor outfit.

Today, the F-22A chief instructor pilot at the 433rd Weapons Squadron, USAF Weapons School, 57th Wing, Nellis Air Force Base, Nevada is in charge of the design and execution of the F-22A Weapons Instructor Course syllabus, producing tactical experts for all the combat air forces.

effort, and members of the 433rd Weapons Squadron reached out to the existing and planned frontline units at Langley, Elmendorf, Holloman, and Tyndall Air Force Bases.

"We can't do this without their expertise," Col Milohnic said. "They are the customers. We're making a huge effort to give them what they want."

The Weapons School then held a validation course for the F-22A programme in January 2009, during which six instructor pilots put one another through the full course, ironing out any bugs. This prepared them for the first actual F-22A Weapons School course, for three students, which began in July 2009. They became Raptor experts, able to carry a standardised message for the employment of the aircraft back to the frontline. The first Raptor Weapons Instructor Officers graduated in June 2009.

The establishment of the F-22A Weapons School course marked real progress in the type's weapons systems maturity. The new F-22 course also marked a step forward in the integration of Air National Guard into the Weapons School, with Maj Fesler serving as the school's first guardsman instructor pilot.

"The torch of air dominance will someday be passed to the F-22," said Lieutenant Colonel

Two Nellis-based Raptors, 'WA'-coded 06-4116 And 'OT'-coded 04-4066 flying in formation with an F-15C. Nellis, Edwards and Tyndall currently operate many of the Block 20 F-16s that are now threatened with early withdrawal. *US Air Force, Senior Airman Kevin Tanenbaum*

The 433rd WPS flagship over the Nevada Test and Training Range, refuelling receptacle doors open on the spine. The US Air Force Weapons School claims to provide the world's most advanced training in weapons and tactics employment. *US Air Force, Senior Airman Kevin Tanenbaum*

# 412th Test Wing

## Edwards AFB, California

**THE 412TH TEST WING** (412 TW) is assigned to the Air Force Test Center at Edwards Air Force Base, California, reporting to Air Force Materiel Command (AFMC). It is the successor unit to the old Air Force Systems Command's 6510th Test Wing, which was redesignated after Systems Command was inactivated in June 1992, becoming the 412th Test Wing on October 2, 1992. The Air Force Flight Test Center was re-designated as the Air Force Test Center on July 13, 2012, and is a cornerstone of AFMC's consolidation initiative from 12 centres to five.

The 412th Test Wing is the host wing for Edwards Air Force Base, the second largest base in the US Air Force, with 10,000 military, federal, and contract personnel based at the 470 square mile installation in the middle of the Mojave Desert. The giant site straddles Kern County, San Bernardino County and Los Angeles County. Edwards proudly proclaims itself to be the: "Center of the Aerospace Testing Universe," and has a long tradition of aircraft and systems testing.

The base was originally established in August 1932, when Lieutenant Colonel Henry H. 'Hap' Arnold began the process of acquiring land next to Muroc Dry Lake to serve as a new bombing range for his 1st Wing at March Field in the increasingly congested Riverside County. Well away from populated areas, the dry lake was so flat (Arnold described it as being: "level as a billiard table") that it was well suited for use as a giant runway, ideal for flight testing. Test flying came to dominate operations at Muroc from 1942, when the base was chosen as a secluded site for testing America's first jet, the Bell Aircraft P-59 Airacomet.

The dry lake was a hive of early hot rodding, with racing on the playa, and aviatrix Florence 'Pancho' Barnes built her renowned Rancho Oro Verde Fly-Inn Dude Ranch (aka 'The Happy Bottom Riding Club') nearby. This became something of a favoured hangout for test pilots, who earned a free steak dinner if and

> *"Florence 'Pancho' Barnes built her renowned Rancho Oro Verde Fly-Inn Dude Ranch (aka 'The Happy Bottom Riding Club') nearby."*

*The F-22 Combined Test Force achieved a sustainability milestone in 2008 when an Edwards-based F-22 Raptor undertook aerial refuelling from a KC-135 Stratotanker from March Air Reserve Base using a synthetic fuel. This was the first time that a US Air Force aircraft had refuelled in flight using an alternative jet engine fuel. The fuel was a 50/50 mix of JP-8 jet fuel and a natural gas-based fuel. US Air Force*

Then the oldest flying F-22 Raptor, tail number 4007, the 412th TW 'flagship', successfully completed its 1,000th sortie on April 19, 2013. The F-22 Combined Test Force celebrated the milestone with a James Bond themed plane-side ceremony, referring to the aircraft's tail number ending in '007'. An older aircraft, 4006, was later returned to flying status! *Lockheed Martin, David Henry*

when they broke the sound barrier for the first time. The club closed in 1953, after a catastrophic fire.

Muroc Field was renamed Muroc Army Airfield and then Muroc Air Force Base before its final renaming in 1950 for USAAF test pilot Captain Glen Edwards. Edwards was recommended as project pilot for the first attempt to exceed the speed of sound in the Bell X-1, an honour that instead went to Captain Chuck Yeager. Edwards was killed in the crash of the Northrop YB-49 at Muroc.

More than US $120m was spent to develop and expand Muroc in the 1940s. The base's main 15,000ft (4,600m) runway was completed in a single pour of concrete.

Notable occurrences at Muroc and Edwards include Chuck Yeager's flight that broke the sound barrier in the Bell X-1, the first test flights of the North American X-15, the first

landings of the Space Shuttle, and the 1986 around-the-world flight of the Rutan Voyager.

The runway on which the Space Shuttle landed follows the track that hosted hot rod racing in the 1930s.

Today, the 412th Test Wing plans, conducts, analyses, and reports on all flight and ground testing of aircraft, weapons systems, software, and components for the USAF as well as modelling and simulation.

As the 6510th Test Wing, the unit received the YF-22A and the YF-23A Advanced Tactical Fighter prototypes for their Dem/Val (Demonstration and Validation) phase.

The 412th Operations Group (412 OG) controls eight flight test squadrons, which are grouped by mission, under the headings Global Power (fighters and bombers), Global Reach (transport and special missions) and Global Vigilance (unmanned).

The F-22 continues to undergo test and evaluation by the wing's 411th Flight Test Squadron (part of the Global Power work stream) – with upgrades and modernisation efforts continuing. Like the wing's other aircraft, the F-22s wear 'ED' (for Edwards) tail codes.

Alongside the F-22s of the 411th Flight Test Squadron, the wing includes the 416th Flight Test Squadron (F-16), the 419th Flight Test Squadron: (B-52H, B-1, and B-2) the 445th Flight Test Squadron: (Initial Flight Test Operations, T-38) and the 461st Flight Test Squadron: (F-35 Lightning II). The 418th Flight Test Squadron looks after Global Reach, and the 452nd Flight Test Squadron is responsible for the Global Vigilance test effort.

The 412th Test Wing also operates the US Air Force Test Pilot School.

# 411th Flight Test Squadron

**THE SQUADRON WAS FIRST** activated as the 6511th Test Squadron in March 1989 to conduct the Advanced Tactical Fighter Dem/Val programme, under which the Lockheed YF-22 and Northrop YF-23 were comparatively evaluated. The unit flew both types through to December 1990, and conducted the Advanced Tactical Fighter fly-off between the two pairs of prototypes.

These aircraft were assigned to the manufacturers rather than to USAF and were primarily flown by industry test pilots. The YF-22 (and the Pratt & Whitney F119 engine) was declared the winner of the competition on April 23, 1991, and on August 2, 1991 both YF-22 prototypes were transferred to the US Air Force.

Though the Number 1 YF-22 returned to the Lockheed Corporation plant to become a ground test bed for production designs, the Number 2 aircraft flew with the 6511th

until April 25, 1992, when it was extensively damaged in a landing mishap.

The 6511th Test Squadron was redesignated as the 411th Test Squadron on October 2, 1992, becoming the 411th Flight Test Squadron on March 1, 1994.

The first of seven F-22A EMD prototypes (91-4001, c/n 4001, named *Spirit of America*) was delivered to Edwards AFB on board a C-5 transport on February 5, 1998. It was re-flown for the first time on May 17, 1998. The second EMD F-22A prototype (91-4002, c/n 4002) flew cross-country to Edwards AFB on August 26, 1998 to join 91-4001 in the test programme.

Thereafter, the six main Engineering and Manufacturing Development (EMD) phase aircraft (4004-4009), were delivered to Edwards for use by the squadron. The first Production Representative Test Vehicle, Raptor number 10 (99-4010), was assigned

to Edwards AFB to serve with the Air Force Operational Test and Evaluation Center to support the Dedicated Initial Operational Test and Evaluation phase.

In recent years, the squadron has operated a smaller number of surviving EMD aircraft (principally 4007, 4009 with 4006 rejoining the programme in 2018) and a Block 30 aircraft, 06-0132.

The commander of the 411th is also the director of the Combined Test Force (CTF) which is an organisational construct that brings together the government developmental test and evaluation personnel, the operational testers, and representatives of the warfighting user community, and the contractors who develop and test the aerospace system, all working together as a team. Members of the CTF formulate the test programme, develop the criteria for flight test missions, execute

*The last of the F-22 EMD batch, 91-4009, is a long-standing and hard-working member of the 411th FLTS fleet at Edwards AFB and is now working on both F-22 and NGAD-related development work, since the Raptor Combined Test Force became the Air Dominance Combined Test Force in June 2023. US Air Force*

> "The convergence of Development Test and Operational Test promises to allow the CTF to test systems against their contracted specification, while simultaneously testing against real-world operational environments."

This F-22 (06-4132) is the 411th Flight Test Squadron 'flagship'. It is seen here taking off from Edwards AFB for a flyover intended to kick off the 2022 MLB All-Star game at Dodger Stadium in Los Angeles, on July 19, 2022. The aircraft carries a pattern of camera calibration markings. *US Air Force, Giancarlo Casem*

flight test missions, analyse data and report on the results. This concept enables a cheaper, faster, and more effective test programme and produces a more effective system for the warfighter.

When Lieutenant Colonel Michael Coleman formally assumed command of the 411th Flight Test Squadron from Lieutenant Colonel David Schmitt on June 9, 2023, what had been the F-22 Raptor Combined Test Force formally transitioned to being the Air Dominance Combined Test Force, tasked with continuing F-22 testing, but also with flight testing the Next Generation Air Dominance (NGAD) Family of Systems.

The Air Dominance CTF will therefore continue to test enhancements for the F-22 to maintain lethality against immediate threats (including some systems which will subsequently be ported to NGAD). It will increasingly work on planning and execution of integrated flight test campaigns for the NGAD Family of Systems.

The new mission will leverage the proven ability of Edwards' units to exploit shared resources across the test enterprise (including representatives from Developmental Test (DT), Operational Test (OT), the programme offices, and support contractors) to ensure the delivery of cutting-edge capability for the warfighter. "In April, we celebrated 70 years of having zero combat losses due to an aerial attack," Coleman said. "This CTF is laser focused on ensuring that legacy continues."

Col Coleman said that: "The establishment of the Air Dominance CTF shows that we are becoming more integrated and more lethal, while also shaping the future of air combat. We do not fight as individual platforms, but rather we leverage a system of systems approach across the entire kill chain. We will be an integral part of fielding a family of innovative platforms and systems through NGAD that will enable the air force to control the skies in a highly contested environment."

The convergence of Development Test and Operational Test promises to allow the CTF to test systems against their contracted specification, while simultaneously testing against real-world operational environments. Its supporters claim this combined test environment promises 'capability delivery at the speed of relevance for the warfighter'.

Edwards-based examples of the F-22, F-35, and F-16 performed the flyover for the MLB All Star games on July 19, 2022. The 2022 Major League Baseball All-Star game (between the American League (AL) and the National League (NL) of Major League Baseball) was hosted by the Los Angeles Dodgers at Dodger Stadium. *US Air Force*

# 49th Fighter Wing

## Holloman Air Force Base, New Mexico

**TODAY, THE 49TH WING** operates F-16s and MQ-9 Reapers from Holloman Air Force Base, New Mexico, primarily in the training role.

Throughout the post-Cold War years, Holloman became the home of the F-117A. When the air force announced that the F-117A Nighthawk would be retired by 2008, Holloman quickly became one of the preferred bases to receive the F-22A Raptor.

The first two F-22s for the 49th Fighter Wing were flown to Holloman on June 2, 2008, and the 5th generation fighter aircraft was officially welcomed during a Total Force Integration Announcement Ceremony, on June 6, 2008, attended by General T. Michael Moseley, the then-chief of staff of the US Air Force.

The ceremony also served as a platform for the announcement that the Air Force Reserve's 301st Fighter Squadron from Luke AFB, Arizona, would form a classic association with the 7th and 8th Fighter Squadrons at Holloman.

After Holloman was selected as a location for an additional Remotely Piloted Aircraft (RPA) Formal Training Unit, the 49th Fighter Wing was redesignated as the 49th Wing on June 30, 2010.

The Total Force Integration between active-duty and reserve airmen became official with the stand up of the 44th Fighter Group, 44th Aircraft Maintenance Squadron and 301st Fighter Squadron on April 9, 2010.

On July 29, 2010, the Pentagon announced that it would deactivate both of Holloman's two F-22 squadrons, the 7th and 8th Fighter Squadrons, as part of an effort to consolidate the F-22 fleet at four bases – Elmendorf in Alaska, Langley in Virginia, Nellis in Nevada, and Tyndall in Florida. This was intended to

At home on the range: The 49th Fighter Wing 'flagship' flying over the Nevada Test and Training Range on March 2, 2011, during a Red Flag training mission. The aircraft was normally based at Holloman Air Force Base, New Mexico. US Air Force, Senior Airman Brett Clashman

enhance F-22 operational flexibility and to maximise combat aircraft and squadrons available for contingencies.

Both of the Holloman units had distinguished histories and had started operating the F-22 in June 2008, but the air force decided to deactivate the 8th Fighter Squadron altogether and transfer the other to Tyndall, where it would become the 95th FS.

The 7th Fighter Squadron was supposed to move its personnel and aircraft to Tyndall Air Force Base in the spring of 2013 to comply with the F-22 fleet consolidation plan, but a Congressionally-enacted freeze on US Air Force structural changes prevented this.

To replace the F-22s, Holloman was supposed to gain two F-16 training squadrons from Luke Air Force Base (making room there for the F-35), but this move was also postponed.

Eventually, the first five F-22 Raptors left Holloman for Tyndall on January 6, 2014, as part of the base's transition from F-22 operations to F-16 Fighting Falcon training.

The final four-ship tactical sortie was flown from Holloman on February 20. Six Raptors left Holloman each month until the move was completed on April 8, 2014.

The 7th Fighter Squadron name remained at Holloman Air Force Base, and the squadron's aircraft and personnel became the 95th Fighter Squadron, a squadron with strong historical links with Tyndall's history.

Airman 1st Class Jonathan Foster, a crew chief from the 49th Aircraft Maintenance Squadron from Holloman Air Force Base, shakes hands with Major Daniel Lehoski a pilot of the 8th Fighter Squadron, before he takes the wing 'flagship' for a training mission during Red Flag 11-3 at Nellis Air Force Base, on March 2, 2011. US Air Force

> *"Eventually, the first five F-22 Raptors left Holloman for Tyndall on January 6, 2014, as part of the base's transition from F-22 operations to F-16 Fighting Falcon training."*

# 7th Fighter Squadron

## 'Screamin' Demons'

**TODAY, THE 7TH FIGHTER** Squadron is assigned to the 1st Operations Group, part of the 1st Fighter Wing at Joint Base Langley-Eustis, Virginia. The squadron operates T-38 Talons to help prepare F-22 Raptor pilots for real-world combat scenarios. The squadron was previously an F-22 operator itself, forming part of the 49th Wing at Holloman.

A long-serving F-117A unit, the 7th Combat Training Squadron was inactivated on December 15, 2006.

The 7th Fighter Squadron was reactivated on May 15, 2008, as the first of two F-22 squadrons to be activated at Holloman AFB. The unit's first F-22A Raptor arrived at Holloman on June 2, 2008. The aircraft was the first of 18 F-22s transferred from the 3rd Wing at Elmendorf Air Force Base, Alaska, and the final aircraft was received in late 2009.

The F-22's career in New Mexico was destined to be brief, cut short by the F-22 fleet consolidation plan. It was announced that the 7th Fighter Squadron was to move its support personnel and aircraft to Tyndall Air Force Base, Florida, where it would 'renumber' as the 95th Fighter Squadron.

The last of the 7th FS F-22s were sent to Tyndall in April 2014, and the squadron was inactivated on May 2 of that year.

The unit was reactivated as the 7th Fighter Training Squadron at Langley on November 12, 2021, taking personnel and equipment transferred from the 71st FTS.

*An F-22A takes off from Holloman Air Force Base on October 22, 2008. Holloman had only a short time as an F-22 base, and the 7th FS had a brief career as an F-22 unit. US Air Force, Technical Sergeant Chris Flahive*

# 8th Fighter Squadron

## 'Black Sheep'

**TODAY, THE 8TH FIGHTER** Squadron is assigned to the 54th Fighter Group, part of Air Education and Training Command, stationed at Holloman Air Force Base, New Mexico and flying the F-16 conducting initial training, transition, and instructor upgrades training roles. It briefly operated the F-22 from 2009-2011.

The 8th inactivated on May 16, 2008 with the departure of the last F-117A Nighthawk from Holloman. The 8th Fighter Squadron was reactivated on September 25, 2009, equipped with the Lockheed Martin F-22 Raptor, joining the 7th Fighter Squadron. The squadron was equipped with 18 F-22s, the last of them being received in 2010.

After less than two years of operating F-22s, it was announced in 2010 that the squadron would stand down as part of the USAF's Raptor fleet consolidation plan. Some of the 8th FS F-22s went to the 7th Fighter Squadron, while others were transferred to the 3rd Wing at Joint Base Elmendorf-Richardson, Alaska; the 1st Fighter Wing at Joint Base Langley-Eustis, Virginia, and the USAF Weapons School at Nellis Air Force Base, Nevada.

The squadron became non-operational in May 2011, and inactivated on July 15, 2011.

*Lieutenant Colonel Craig Baker, 8th Fighter Squadron commander, taxies into a hangar in the first F-22 Raptor assigned to the 8th FS (04-4077), on December 21, 2009. Colonel Baker assumed command of the squadron on September 25. The 8th has not had any aircraft assigned to it since the F-117 retired in April 2008. US Air Force, Senior Airman John D. Strong II*

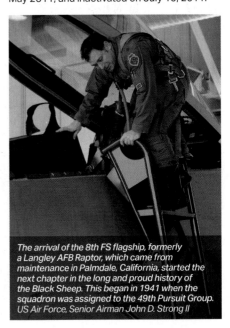

*The arrival of the 8th FS flagship, formerly a Langley AFB Raptor, which came from maintenance in Palmdale, California, started the next chapter in the long and proud history of the Black Sheep. This began in 1941 when the squadron was assigned to the 49th Pursuit Group. US Air Force, Senior Airman John D. Strong II*

# 325th Fighter Wing
## Tyndall Air Force Base, Florida

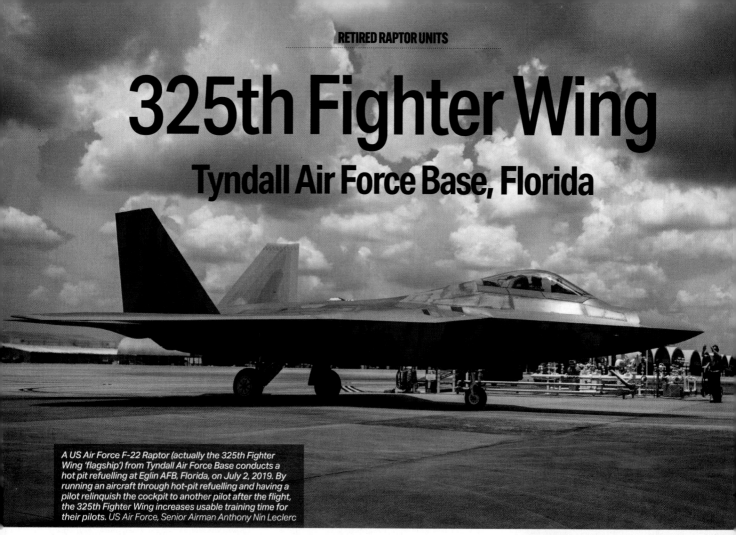

A US Air Force F-22 Raptor (actually the 325th Fighter Wing 'flagship') from Tyndall Air Force Base conducts a hot pit refuelling at Eglin AFB, Florida, on July 2, 2019. By running an aircraft through hot-pit refuelling and having a pilot relinquish the cockpit to another pilot after the flight, the 325th Fighter Wing increases usable training time for their pilots. US Air Force, Senior Airman Anthony Nin Leclerc

**THE 325TH FIGHTER WING** (325 FW) is a wing of the United States Air Force notionally based at Tyndall Air Force Base, Florida, but currently operating from Eglin.

The wing's primary mission is to provide air dominance training for F-22 Raptor pilots and maintenance personnel and air battle managers to support the combat air force.

F-22 pilot training was performed by the 43rd Fighter Squadron, though this is in the process of transitioning to the 71st Fighter Squadron at Langley. The wing continues to provide mission-ready F-22 air dominance forces in support of the Commander, North American Aerospace Defense Command (NORAD)/1st Air Force (1 AF) contingency plans, though the 95th Fighter Squadron has been reduced to a cadre, and the 301st is preparing to convert to the F-35A.

The 325th Fighter Wing added the 43d Fighter Squadron to conduct F-22 training in 2003, initially in addition to its F-15C/D training mission. The 325th FW conducted both F-15C/D and F-22A training until 2010, when the 173rd Fighter Wing assumed the F-15C/D FTU role for both the regular air force and the Air National Guard.

The 325th has conducted the USAF's basic course and transition training for the F-22 since 2003, training pilots from the regular air force, Air Force Reserve Command (AFRC) and the Air National Guard (ANG).

> **"The 325th has conducted the USAF's basic course and transition training for the F-22 since 2003."**

The wing was reassigned from Air Education and Training Command (AETC) to Air Combat Command (ACC) in October 2012, gaining a combat coded F-22 squadron by reactivating the 95th Fighter Squadron (95 FS) on October 11, 2013.

The 2nd Fighter Training Squadron was reactivated In August 2014, flying the Northrop T-38 Talon to provide adversary training support to the Wing's F-22 squadrons.

In the wake of Hurricane Michael in 2018, F-22 and T-38 flight training operations were moved from Tyndall to the recently vacated US Navy F-35C training facility at Eglin AFB. The combat-coded F-22A aircraft of the 95 FS were redistributed to other F-22 units in Virginia, Hawaii, and Alaska and the squadron was reduced to cadre status.

In 2021, after more than two years of speculation, the air force announced that the 325th would be re-equipped with the F-35A Lightning II, with three F-35 squadrons, totalling 72 aircraft. The first of the F-35A aircraft are due to begin arriving at Tyndall in September or October 2023.

A 43rd Fighter Squadron pilot from Tyndall Air Force Base, briefs the next pilot to fly the aircraft after hot pit refuelling at Eglin AFB. If the aircraft didn't record anything unsafe during flight, the next pilot can take it on another flight without turning the jet over to maintenance. US Air Force, Senior Airman Anthony Nin Leclerc

# 43rd Fighter Squadron

## 'Hornets'

**THE 43RD FIGHTER SQUADRON** is part of the 325th Fighter Wing, notionally based at Tyndall Air Force Base, Florida, but operating from Eglin since Hurricane Michael. The eastern part of the Gulf of Mexico has provided invaluable airspace for air dominance training. The squadron remained responsible for providing conversion and air dominance training for the F-22 Raptor until 2023, when the role transitioned to Langley.

The squadron is one of the oldest in the United States Air Force, its origins dating to June 13, 1917, when it was organised at Kelly Field, Texas as the 43rd Aero Squadron. The squadron deployed to England as part of the American Expeditionary Force during World War One. It also saw combat during World War Two, served in the Vietnam war and later became part of the Alaskan Air Command (AAC) during the Cold War.

The 43rd Fighter Squadron was reactivated on October 25, 2002, and, as the first training squadron for US Air Force pilots destined for the F-22 Raptor, was also the first squadron to receive the F-22.

Originally assigned to the 325th Fighter Wing, Air Education and Training Command, at Tyndall Air Force Base, Florida, the squadron transitioned to Air Combat Command in October 2012, when the 325th Fighter Wing assumed an operational mission, although the 43rd FS continued in its training role.

In the aftermath of Hurricane Michael, the F-22 Formal Training Unit mission left Tyndall for Eglin, though students and instructors had to navigate a significant geographical

*Where necessary, an instructor pilot will 'chase' his student in another Raptor. Here two 43rd FS F-22As (the 325th FW 'flagship' and 02-4033) fly over the Florida coastline on November 12, 2008. US Air Force*

separation between the academic and simulation portions of the course – which remained at Tyndall – and the flying parts of the syllabus. But despite this, and despite a global COVID-19 pandemic, the 43rd FS managed to expand the B-Course from 28 graduates per year to 30, meeting headquarters' requirements for the first time.

While the 325th Fighter Wing's mission transitions from F-22 training to F-35 warfighting, the F-22 B-Course has started to move to Joint Base Langley-Eustis, Virginia.

The final class graduated by the 43rd Fighter Squadron, was class 23-ABR, which consisted of eight student pilots. As well as celebrating their graduation, the 43rd Fighter Squadron dispatched an initial pair of aircraft to Langley for the new FTU, the 71st Fighter Squadron. For this flight, the two aircraft emerged onto Tyndall's flight line bearing the 1st Fighter Wing's 'FF' tail code as they departed for their new home.

Since its beginning, the 43rd Fighter Squadron has produced 830 Raptor pilots.

*Tyndall training birds in flight, with a T-38 Talon (68-8185) trailing two veteran F-22s, with 01-4019 (an LRIP Lot 1 aircraft, the second delivered to the USAF) leading 02-4034. Team Tyndall achieved their 25,000th F-22 sortie during a 43rd Fighter Squadron basic course training mission on October 7, 2013, the very day that this photo was taken. US Air Force*

# 95th Fighter Squadron

## 'Boneheads'

**THE 95TH FIGHTER SQUADRON** (95th FS), nicknamed the Boneheads, is an active United States Air Force F-35A squadron.

It was previously a frontline, F-22 equipped squadron, but in the aftermath of Hurricane Michael on October 10, 2018 and the destruction of large parts of Tyndall Air Force Base, the squadron's aircraft and personnel were distributed to other duty stations across the F-22 Raptor fleet, and it was reduced to a cadre.

The squadron was activated as an F-22 unit at Tyndall on October 11, 2013 as a combat-coded Lockheed Martin F-22 Raptor unit under the 325th Operations Group. The unit received aircraft from the disbanding 7th Fighter Squadron at Holloman Air Force Base beginning in January 2014. The 95th completed acceptance of its complement of aircraft and achieved initial operational capability in April 2014.

The 95th FS and other elements of the 325th Fighter Wing completed their first six-month long combat deployment with the Raptor in May 2015 as part of Operation Inherent Resolve.

In October 2018, when large parts of Tyndall Air Force Base were damaged by Hurricane Michael, Tyndall's flying units were relocated to other bases, with the 2nd Fighter Training Squadron and 43rd Fighter Squadron being relocated to Eglin Air Force Base, Florida, while

the aircraft and personnel of the 95th Fighter Squadron were split up and relocated to Joint Base Elmendorf–Richardson, Alaska, Joint Base Langley–Eustis, Virginia, and Joint Base Pearl Harbor–Hickam, Hawaii. The squadron was subsequently disbanded in 2019.

The 95th Fighter Squadron activated on June 15, 2023 as a Lockheed Martin F-35 squadron, again stationed at Tyndall AFB. The unit is scheduled to receive its first F-35A Lightning II aircraft in August 2023.

*An F-22 Raptor pilot assigned to the 95th Fighter Squadron exits an F-22 at Spangdahlem Air Base, Germany, on August 28, 2015. The US Air Force deployed four F-22 Raptors, one C-17 Globemaster III and more than 50 airmen to Spangdahlem in support of the first F-22 European training deployment. The deployment was funded by the European Reassurance Initiative, a $1bn pledge announced by President Obama in March 2014. US Air Force, Airman 1st Class Luke Kitterman*

*An F-22 Raptor with the 95th Fighter Squadron, Tyndall Air Force Base, Florida, waits to refuel beside a KC-135 Stratotanker over the Nevada Test and Training Range on January 28, 2016, during exercise Red Flag-16-1. The Tanker Task Force for Red Flag 16-1 involved KC-135 Stratotankers from MacDill Air Force Base, and McConnell Air Force Base. US Air Force, Master Sergeant Burt Traynor*

*"The 95th FS and other elements of the 325th Fighter Wing completed their first six-month long combat deployment with the Raptor in May 2015."*

# 301st Fighter Squadron

*An African American formation flying over Alabama on September 6, 2018, honouring the Tuskegee Airmen past, present and future. Here the Commemorative Air Force P-51C Mustang (wearing wartime 332nd Fighter Group markings) was piloted by CAF member and Tuskegee Airman descendant Brad Lang, with a 100th Fighter Squadron, Alabama ANG F-16 piloted by Major Rich 'Sheriff' Peace and a 301st Fighter Squadron F-22 piloted by Major Paul 'Loco' Lopez. US Air Force, Staff Sergeant Clayton Cupit*

*Lieutenant Colonel Randall Cason, 301st Fighter Squadron commander, stands in front of an F-22 Raptor at Tyndall AFB. In 2006, Cason had become the first Air Force Reserve pilot to fly the F-22. US Air Force, Airman 1st Class Sergio A. Gamboa*

**THE 301ST FIGHTER SQUADRON** flies the F-22 Raptor as an associate unit of the active duty 325th Fighter Wing. The squadron is assigned to the 325th Operations Group, notionally stationed at Tyndall Air Force Base, Florida. It reports to the 44th Fighter Group (44th FG). The 44th FG itself is a component of the AFRC 301st Fighter Wing, based at Carswell Field, Naval Air Station Fort Worth Joint Reserve Base, Texas.

When Hurricane Michael devastated Tyndall Air Force Base in 2018, F-22 operations were relocated to Eglin AFB.

The 301st Fighter Squadron originally stood up as an F-22 unit at Holloman AFB, alongside and as part of Air Force Reserve Command's 44th Fighter Group, on April 9, 2010. Two F-22 Raptors were on show, one of which was decorated with a 44th FG tail flash and one with a 301st FS tail flash. The unit became Air Combat Command's only reserve F-22 Raptor unit.

The squadron's role was to provide advanced fighter training as a reserve corollary unit to the 49th Fighter Wing, though its time at Holloman was brief.

The squadron activated at Tyndall AFB, Florida on October 1, 2012, where it formed a classic association with the 325th Fighter Wing and supported the operational F-22 Raptor combat-coded AETC training unit mission at Tyndall. As it was at Holloman, the 301st Fighter Squadron remained part of the 44th Fighter Group.

In August 2016, Total Force Initiative Airmen assigned to the active-duty 95th and Reserve 301st Fighter Squadrons from Tyndall AFB, participated in exercises Combat Hammer and Combat Archer, testing their ability to build, load, launch and employ munitions. These exercises were conducted at Hill Air Force Base and the Utah Test and Training Range.

During the exercises, the Tyndall F-22s dropped 32 precision guided munitions, employed 14 air-to-air missiles, and validated AIM-9X missile employment procedures, a first for the Tyndall Raptor units.

When Tyndall sustained a direct hit from Hurricane Michael in 2018, it caused massive damage, and led to a relocation of F-22 operations to Eglin AFB. Construction is now underway to rebuild the base and shape it into the US Air Force's first 21st century 'Installation of the Future'. Tyndall is on the road to becoming fully operational and plans to welcome F-35 Lightning II aircraft beginning September 2023.

The 44 FG is currently (July 2023) still executing its mission of producing 5th generation combat capability at Eglin with the F-22 FTU mission but is looking forward to transitioning back to Tyndall to continue the 5th generation mission by integrating with the 325th FW to provide combat F-35 units to the CAF.

The 301st Fighter Wing was selected to receive AFRC's first ever F-35A mission and is transitioning from the F-16 Fighting Falcon to the F-35. As a geographically separated unit of the 301 FW, the 44 FG will also transition from the F-22 to the F-35 and has been already supporting the 33 FW's F-35 mission. This valuable experience will help the 44th FG's F-35 cadre team make the transition when they move back to Tyndall AFB.

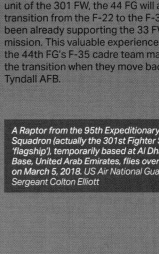

*A Raptor from the 95th Expeditionary Fighter Squadron (actually the 301st Fighter Squadron 'flagship'), temporarily based at Al Dhafra Air Base, United Arab Emirates, flies over Syria on March 5, 2018. US Air National Guard, Staff Sergeant Colton Elliott*

# Raptor Chronology

## The key dates in the F-22 Raptor's development and deployment as the world's first fifth-gen fighter aircraft.

### 1980 ON...

**1981:** ATF requirement issued

**May 1981:** RFI issued

**November 1981:** USAF formally identifies requirement for new air superiority fighter to replace F-15

**September 1983:** USAF awards concept definition contracts to seven manufacturers for ATF **September 1983:** Engine DemVal contracts awarded to Pratt & Whitney and General Electric

**September 1985:** DemVal RFP issued

**October 1985:** Lockheed Model 090P design configuration frozen

**November 1985:** USAF issues more stringent stealth goals for ATF designs

**May 1986:** SecAF says that ATF DemVal phase must include prototype aircraft, engines, and avionics

**June 1986:** USAF awards prototype engine contracts to Pratt & Whitney and General Electric for YF119-PW-100 and YF120-GE-100, respectively

**June 27, 1986:** Lockheed, Boeing, & General Dynamics sign teaming agreement MoU

**October 13, 1986:** Formal ATF Teaming Agreement signed by Lockheed, General Dynamics, and Boeing

**October 31, 1986:** Lockheed-Boeing-General Dynamics team and Northrop-McDonnell Douglas teams selected to participate in ATF DemVal phase

**July 17, 1987:** Initial tests of YF-22 avionics on 757 Airborne Flying Laboratory

**October 1987:** Configuration 614 (with diamond wing and four tail) is selected

**November 1987:** Tail configuration modified

### 1990 ON...

**1990:** Major aircraft review, reduced planned total from 750 to 648 aircraft

**January 13, 1990:** YF-22 PAV-1 final assembly begins in Palmdale

**April 1990:** YF-22 PAV-2 final assembly begins

**August 1990:** F-22 EMD configuration frozen

**August 29, 1990:** YF-22A PAV-1, powered by General Electric YF120-GE-100 turbofans, unveiled at Lockheed Plant 10 in Palmdale

**September 29, 1990:** YF-22 PAV-1 first flight by Dave Ferguson from Palmdale to the Edwards AFB

**October 25, 1990:** Maj. Mark Shackelford becomes first USAF pilot to fly the YF-22. This flight is first YF-22 supersonic flight

**October 26, 1990:** First aerial refuelling of the YF-22

**November 3, 1990:** First YF-22 supercruise, by PAV-1

**November 15, 1990:** YF-22 PAV-1 demonstrates thrust vectoring

**November 23, 1990:** First Pratt & Whitney YF-22 PAV-2 supercruise

**November 28, 1990:** First YF-22 live missile firing by General Dynamics test pilot Jon Beesley, flying PAV-2, at China Lake

**December 10, 1990:** PAV-1 High angle-of-attack testing begins

**December 11, 1990:** First YF-22 formation flight

**December 17, 1990:** YF-22 high angle-of-attack testing completed. YF-22 attains an unprecedented 60° angle-of-attack and remains in full control

**December 20, 1990:** First AIM-120 firing. By Tom Morgenfeld in PAV-2 over the Pacific Missile Test Range at Point Mugu

**December 28, 1990:** Mach 2 achieved by Tom Morgenfeld in PAV-1

**December 28, 1990:** DemVal flight test phase ends after 74 sorties (91.6 hours)

**April 22, 1991:** Air Force Secretary Dr Donald Rice announces the number of ATFs to be procured will be reduced from 750 to 648 aircraft

**April 1991:** Lockheed/PW announced as winners of ATF competition

**June 1991:** PAV-1 air-freighted to Andrews AFB, Maryland, to participate in the Air Force's Stealth Week exhibit for congress and the media

**August 2, 1991:** US Air Force awards $9.55bn contract to Lockheed-Boeing-General Dynamics team to begin F-22 EMD phase. Covers 11 flyable aircraft (nine single-seat F-22As and two tandem-seat F-22Bs), one static test and one fatigue test airframe. Separate $1.4bn contract to Pratt & Whitney to build 33 engines

**October 30, 1991:** PAV-2 flight testing resumes at Edwards AFB

**December 16, 1991:** External design of the F-22 frozen

**April 25, 1992:** PAV-2 (N22YX) damaged in take-off accident

**June 4, 1992:** F-22 design review update completed

**January 1993:** F-22 EMD programme schedule is rephased, EMD fleet reduced from 11 to nine (still includes two F-22B trainers)

**February 10, 1994:** Bottom Up Review reduced planed total from 648 to 442 aircraft

**February 24, 1995:** Critical Design Review completed, marking end of detailed design phase, and ensuring readiness for fabrication and assembly

**March 15, 1995:** Lockheed Corporation and Martin Marietta complete a "merger of equals" becoming Lockheed Martin Corporation

**April 20, 1995:** USAF awards $9.5m , 24 month study contract for F-22 derivatives

**July 1995:** 16,930 test hour wind tunnel testing programme of F-22 configuration completed

**February 1996:** Tests of the flight control laws begin in VISTA F-16

**July 10, 1996:** USAF defers requirement for design and development of two-seat F-22B. Two planned EMD F-22s replaced by two single-seat F-22As

**April 9, 1997:** First F-22 (4001) unveiled and named Raptor

**1997:** Production reduced to 339 aircraft

**September 7, 1997:** 58 minute first flight by Paul Metz, from Marietta/Dobbins ARB

**September 14, 1997:** Second flight by Jon Beesley - the only pilot to fly both the YF-22 and production F-22

**February 5, 1998:** Raptor 01 flown to Air Force Flight Test Center at Edwards AFB, California, aboard C-5 Galaxy

**May 17, 1998:** Raptor first flight at Edwards AFB, by Lt. Col. Steve Rainey

**July 10, 1998:** Two contracts for advanced procurement and program support for 2 F-22 PRTV aircraft and 6 initial production F-22s (later PRTV II)

**July 30, 1998:** First F-22 AAR, flying from Air Force Flight Test Center at Edwards AFB

**August 26, 1998:** Lt. Col. Steve Rainey delivers Raptor 02 nonstop from Marietta to Edwards AFB

**October 10, 1998:** First F-22 supersonic flight. Jon Beesley reaches Mach 1.1 at 29,000 feet in Raptor 01 (Flight 31)

**November 23, 1998:** Lt. Col. David Nelson USAF flies Congressionally mandated 183rd flying hour required to release funds for Lot 1 production F-22s

**March 11, 1999:** Boeing begins testing the F-22 Block 1 avionics software package aboard the 757 Flying Test Bed

**May 4, 1999:** Raptor 02 flies programme's 100th flight test sortie in the hands of Jon Beesley

**July 20, 1999:** Col. C.D. Moore USAF achieves Mach 1.5 in Raptor 01

**August 25, 1999:** Raptor 02 achieves 60° angle of attack

**November 18, 1999:** F-22 is refuelled from a KC-10 Extender tanker

### 2000 ON...

**July 25, 2000:** First AIM-9 Sidewinder missile launch at China Lake by Boeing Test Pilot Chuck Killberg in Raptor 02

**October 24, 2000:** First AIM-120 AMRAAM launch by Lt. Col. David Nelson in Raptor 02

**November 2, 2000:** Raptor 01 retired to Wright-Patterson AFB for live-fire testing

**November 15, 2000:** First flight of F-22 with a full-up avionics suite (Raptor 04) by Bret Luedke

**April 17, 2001:** Paul Metz launches AIM-9 while rolling at 60° per second. 100°/sec launch achieved on June 13, 2001

**May 17, 2001:** Maximum Mach (Mach 2+) achieved by Col. Gary Plumb in Raptor 03 21

**September 2001:** First guided AIM-120 AMRAAM missile launch in Raptor 05

**February 1, 2002:** Lt. Col. David Nelson pulls 9g in Raptor 03

**July 25, 2002:** First supersonic (Mach 1.11) missile launch (AIM-9) by Lt. Col. Chris Short in Raptor 03 at China Lake

**August 21, 2002:** First supersonic AIM-120 separation test at Mach 1.19 by Lt. Col. Eddie Cabrera in Raptor 03

**September 17, 2002:** Re-designated F/A-22

**October 25, 2002:** 43rd FS reactivated as F-22 FTU

**October 2002:** First production aircraft delivered to Edwards AFB for IOT&E

**November 5, 2002:** First guided supersonic AIM-120 launch by Maj. Jim Dutton in Raptor 07

**2003:** Production reduced to 277 aircraft – limited by Congressional cost cap

**January 14, 2003:** First aircraft to 422nd TES at Nellis AFB (00-4012)

**January 17, 2003:** Lt. Col. David Rose is first operational Air Force pilot to fly the F/A-22 at Nellis AFB

**February 19, 2003:** Col. Ric Cazessus and Lt. Col. Art McGettrick in Raptors 06 and 07 demonstrate Intraflight Data Link

**February 22, 2003:** Lockheed test pilot James Brown fires M61A2 Gatling-gun in flight for first time

**March 4, 2003:** First Raptor for Dedicated Initial Operational Test and Evaluation delivered to Edwards AFB

**August 29, 2003:** First four-ship test of IFDL. Seven Raptors airborne for the first time

**September 26, 2003:** First aircraft delivery to Tyndall for pilot training (01-4018) by Lt. Col. Jeffrey 'Cobra' Harrigian

**November 24, 2003:** Lt. Col. Evan Thomas in Raptor 05 downs a QF-4 drone with an AIM-120 missile at White Sands. Lt. Col. Art McGettrick in Raptor 07 downs a QF-4 drone with an AIM-9M Sidewinder at the Point Mugu

**2004:** Production reduced to 183 aircraft (USAF requirement still stated to be 361)

**January 14, 2004:** Maj. Michael Hoepfner is first pilot to complete F/A-22 transition training with the 43rd FS at Tyndall

**March 19, 2004:** Lt. Col. Evan Thomas ripple fires two AIM-120 AMRAAM missiles from Raptor 07

**April 23, 2004:** First separation test of 1,000lb GBU-32 JDAM by Lt. Col. Evan Thomas in Raptor 03

**April 29, 2004:** IOT&E began

**July 24, 2004:** Col. Joe Lanni ripple fires four AIM-120 AMRAAM missiles from Raptor 05

**September 2004:** IOT&E completed (186 sorties)

**September 2, 2004:** First complete mission demonstration of the Raptor's air-to-ground capability using JDAM (00-4016)

**October 26, 2004:** Raptor 00-4016 ripple releases two guided GBU-32 JDAMs hitting two targets several miles apart

**December 20, 2004:** First loss, 00-4014 crashed on take-off due to FCS malfunction, pilot ejected

**2005:** Follow On OT&E for air-to-ground role

**January 2005:** First combat ready aircraft flown to Langley AFB by 27th Fighter Squadron commander Lt. Col. James Hecker (Aircraft 02-4029 loaned from 325th Fighter Wing)

**January 28, 2005:** First sortie from Langley by a Langley-based pilot (Major Charles 'Corky' Corcoran, of the 27th Fighter Squadron)

**March 29, 2005:** Full rate production approved

**2005:** Increment 2 integrated (JDAM)

**July 14, 2005:** First supersonic JDAM release by Maj. John Teichert of the 411th FLTS in 4008

**August 29, 2005:** Members of the 422nd Test and Evaluation Squadron at Nellis AFB fly the first F/A-22 Follow-on Operational Test and Evaluation mission

**October 15, 2005:** F/A-22s from the 27th FS at Langley deploy to Hill AFB, for first Combat Hammer Exercise by an operational F/A-22 squadron. Exercise includes the first supersonic JDAM drop by an operational squadron

**December 15, 2005:** ISD, re-designated F-22

**December 2005:** F-22 engineering and manufacturing development phase is completed after 3,496 flights and more than 7,600 flying hours

**21 January 2006:** F-22s from the 27th FS at Langley AFB perform Operation Noble Eagle missions

**14 April 2006:** F-22 Combined Test Force at Edwards AFB carries out first flight test of improved AIM-120D AMRAAM

**23 May 2006:** 1st Fighter Wing at Langley deploys 12 Raptors, 18 pilots, and 174 maintainers of 27th FS to Elmendorf AFB for six weeks. During the deployment, F-22s, working with F-15s and F/A-18s, produces a kill ratio of 83 to one in one day. One F-22 pilot achieves nine aerial victories on a single mission

**2006:** Awarded Collier Trophy

**February 2007:** Participated in Exercise Red Flag 07-1

**February 16 - May 11, 2007:** First overseas deployment by 27th FS to Kadena AB, Japan via Hickam. 12 aircraft fly more than 600 sorties during the three-month deployment

**March 2007:** AN/APG-77(V)1 certified

**June 20, 2007:** 192nd Fighter Wing, Virginia Air National Guard unit becomes the first Guard unit to fly the F-22

**September 5, 2007:** First release of 250lb GBU-38 SDB by Maj. Jack Fischer from Raptor 08

**October 2, 2007:** 477th Fighter Group (and the 302nd Fighter Squadron) activated at Elmendorf AFB as first Air Force Reserve Command F-22 unit

**November 2007:** Cold weather testing at Eielson AFB, Alaska

**November 22, 2007:** F-22s of 90th Fighter Squadron at Elmendorf AFB, Alaska, undertook the F-22's first live North American Aerospace Defense Command (NORAD) interception of two Russian Tu-95MS bombers

**December 2, 2007:** F-22 achieved Full Operational Capability (FOC), with 1st Fighter Wing and Virginia Air National Guard 192d Fighter Wing declared fully operational

**2008:** Production increased to 187 production aircraft

**April 2008:** Operational Readiness Inspection (ORI) of the integrated wing - rated "excellent" in all categories, with a simulated kill-ratio of 221–0

**June 6, 2008:** 49th Wing stands up at Holloman AFB

**July 11, 2008:** First supersonic release of a 250lb GBU-39 by the 411th Flight Test Squadron

**August 28, 2008:** 411th FLTS undertook first ever air-to-air refuelling receiving synthetic jet fuel

**2009:** First deployment to Centcom, to Al Dhafra AB, UAE

**March 25, 2009:** An EMD F-22 crashed 35 miles (56 km) northeast of Edwards AFB during a test flight.

Lockheed Martin test pilot David P. Cooley lost consciousness during a high-G manoeuvre then ejected, but was killed during ejection by blunt-force trauma from windblast due to the aircraft's speed

**April 6, 2009:** Robert Gates called for production cap of 187 aircraft, with production ending in FY2011

## 2010 ON…

**May 19, 2010:** First ripple release of 4 GBU-39 SDBs by Maj. Drew Allen, 411th FLTS 16 November 2010, an F-22 from Elmendorf AFB crashed, killing the pilot, Captain Jeffrey Haney, after a bleed air system malfunction shut down the Environmental Control System (ECS) and OBOGS

**July 9, 2010:** Joint Base Pearl Harbor-Hickam, inaugurated as base for the 199th Fighter Squadron, Hawaii Air National Guard

**July 29, 2010:** The Air Force announces F-22 fleet consolidation

**November 16, 2010:** 06-4125 crashed – Capt. Jeffrey Haney failed to eject from the aircraft prior to impact

**January-November 2011:** Final operational testing and evaluation (FOT&E)

**March 18, 2011:** An F-22 flew supersonically with a 50% biofuel mix

**May 3, 2011- September 19, 2011:** Four-month precautionary stand down after 12 reported hypoxic events

**May 13, 2011:** 8th FS inactivated

**November 4, 2011:** Lt. Col. David Piffarerio, of the 302nd Fighter Squadron becomes the first pilot to reach 1,000 flying hours in the F-22

**December 13, 2011:** The final F-22 Raptor (10-4195) is rolled off the assembly line at Marietta

**April 2012:** 3rd Wing conducted the first large-scale exercise with Increment 3.1 aircraft dropping eight live and 12 inert JDAM

**May 2, 2012:** Last aircraft (10-4195) delivered

**July 30, 2012:** First supersonic AIM-9X launch by Maj. Ryan Howland of the F-22 Combined Test Force at Edwards AFB

**August 2012:** Alaska F-22 Raptors became the first operational F-22 unit to drop GBU-39 small diameter bombs (during Combat Hammer exercise)

**September 11, 2012:** 90th Fighter Squadron deploy to Andersen Air Force Base, Guam

**November 15, 2012:** During a training mission, an F-22 (00-4013) crashed to the east of Tyndall AFB, when a 'chafed' electrical wire ignited the fluid in a hydraulic line, causing a fire that damaged the flight controls. The pilot ejected safely

**October 2013:** 95th FS reactivated

**January 6, 2014:** 95th FS's first Raptors arrived from Holloman, continued through to April

**May 2, 2014:** 7th FS inactivated

**September 22/23, 2014:** Raptor combat debut, 27th FS Raptors dropping JDAMs on Daesh targets near the Tishrin Dam in Syria

**September 2014-July 2015:** 95th FS flew 172 operational sorties, dropping 150 munitions

**August 2015:** 95th FS Deployed to Spangdahlem (Germany), Lask (Poland) and Amari (Estonia)

**April 2016:** House Armed Services Committee (HASC) Tactical Air and Land Forces Subcommittee directs production restart study

**April 2016:** 95th Fighter Squadron deploy 12 F-22A Raptors to RAF Lakenheath, with ACE deployments to Mihail Kogalniceanu Air Base, Romania, and Siauliai Air Base, Lithuania

**November 17, 2017:** 95th FS F-22s bombed opium production and storage facilities in Taliban-controlled regions of Afghanistan

**February 7, 2018:** F-22s attacked Russian Wagner Group paramilitary forces near Khasham in eastern Syria

**August 2018:** Lockheed Martin proposed an F-22 derivative with the avionics and improved stealth coatings of the F-35 to the USAF and JASDF

**August 2018:** 95th FS deploy to Spangdahlem Air Base, Germany

**October 2018:** Tyndall aircraft evacuated to Wright Patterson AFB, and later Langley

**October 10, 2018:** Hurricane Michael hits Tyndall
**November 16, 2018:** Last repaired Tyndall aircraft flown out

## 2020 ON…

**May 15, 2020:** An F-22 from Eglin Air Force Base (01-4022) crashed after take-off during a routine training mission after an aircraft wash resulted in faulty air data sensor readings. The pilot ejected safely

**February 2022:** 27th Fighter Squadron deploy to Al Dhafra AB, UAE

**August 4, 2022:** 90th Fighter Squadron deploy to the 32nd Tactical Air Base at Łask in Poland

**November 4, 2022:** 3rd Wing F-22s deploy to Kadena

**February 4, 2023:** An F-22 of the 1st Fighter Wing shot down an alleged Chinese spy balloon off the coast of South Carolina at an altitude of 60-65,000 ft

**February 10, 2023:** F-22s shot down unidentified high-altitude object near the coast of Alaska

**February 11, 2023:** F-22s shot down another high-altitude object over Yukon

**March 29, 2023:** First F-22 Raptors join incoming Formal Training Unit fleet at Joint Base Langley-Eustis

**March 2023:** 525th Fighter Squadron deploy to Tinian, with ACE deployment to Clark Field

**April 2023:** 94th FS deployed to Powidz, and made ACE deployment to Ämari Air Base, Estonia, May 8, 2023

**June 14, 2023:** 94th Fighter Squadron deployed 4+ Raptors to Muwaffaq Salti Air Base in Jordan in response to Russian provocation

**July 2023:** 19th and 199th FS deploy to RAAF Tindal for Talisman Sabre

# F-22 Production Blocks and Totals

EMD aircraft, two production representative test aircraft and 72 Block 10/20 aircraft for training and 112 combat-coded Block 30/35 aircraft.

The EMD and PRTV aircraft, Block 10 and 20 aircraft from LRIP Lots 1, 2 and 3, were upgraded to a common Block 20 configuration under the Common Configuration Program (CCP), with additional computer memory, faster processors and new power supplies giving increased processing capability.

All but six Block 20 aircraft from Lot 3 onward were subsequently upgraded to Block 30 standards, increasing the Block 30/35 fleet to 149 aircraft, with 37 remaining in the Block 20 configuration.

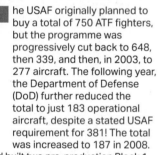

*F-22A 91-4001, marked as Raptor 01, seen during its first flight on September 7, 1997, flown by Paul Metz. The two Demval YF-22s aside, 4001 was the first production configuration Raptor.*
Lockheed Martin

The USAF originally planned to buy a total of 750 ATF fighters, but the programme was progressively cut back to 648, then 339, and then, in 2003, to 277 aircraft. The following year, the Department of Defense (DoD) further reduced the total to just 183 operational aircraft, despite a stated USAF requirement for 381! The total was increased to 187 in 2008. Lockheed built two pre-production Block 1 aircraft, a single Block 2, and then six Block 10

*Some 14 years later, the final F-22A Raptor to be built for the US Air Force, tail number 10-4195, was ceremonially rolled out at Lockheed Martin Aeronautics' assembly line at Marietta on December 13, 2011.*
Lockheed Martin

| Serials | No. and standard | LOT | Notes |
|---|---|---|---|
| 87-0700 to -0701 | 2 x YF-22A | | N22YF and N22YX |
| 91-4001 to -4002 | 2 x Block 1 | EMD/Test. | 91-4001 *Spirit of America*, -4002 *Old Reliable* |
| 91-4003 | 1 x Block 2 | EMD/Test | Structurally representative of production |
| 91-4004 to -4008 | 5 x Block 10 | EMD/Test. | 91-4004 first with fully integrated avionics, 91-4006 to Block 20 |
| 91-4009 | 1 x Block 10 | EMD/Test | |
| 99-4010 to -4011 | 2 x Block 10 | PRTV | Dedicated IOT&E aircraft. Originally 99-4006 to -4007 once intended as two-seat F-22Bs |
| 00-4012 to -4017 | 6 x Block 10 | PRTV II | First production aircraft |
| 01-4018 to -4027 | 10 x Block 10 | LRIP Lot 1 | |
| 02-4028 to -4040 | 13 x Block 10 | LRIP Lot 2 | |
| 03-4041 to -4061 | 21 x Block 20 | LRIP Lot 3 | |
| 04-4062 to -4083 | 22 x Block 20 | Lot 4 | 04-4065 and -4070 were the 'chrome' Raptors, 04-4082 *Cripes A'Mighty* |
| 05-4084 to -4107 | 24 x Block 30 | Lot 5 | |
| 06-4108 to -4130 | 23 x Block 30 | Lot 6 | |
| 07-4131 to -4151 | 21 x Block 30 | Lot 7 | 07-4132 flight sciences aircraft, 146 stored? 07-4147 *Spirit of Tuskegee* |
| 08-4152 to -4171 | 20 x Block 35 | Lot 8 | 08-153 *Arizona Balloon Buster*, 08-4165 *Black Falcon*, 08-4170 *Banzai Betty* |
| 09-4172 to -4191 | 20 x Block 35 | Lot 9 | 09-4172 *Executive Sweet*, 09-4174 *Maloney's Pony* |
| 10-4192 to -4195 | 4 x Block 30 | | Notionally Block 40 - to replace unspecified losses of other aircraft |